COOL CAREERS WITHOUT COLLEGE FOR
PEOPLE
WHO LOVE
TO BUILD
THINGS

COOL CAREERS WITHOUT COLLEGE FOR PEOPLE WHO LOVE TO BUILD THINGS

JOY PAIGE

The Rosen Publishing Group, Inc.

To Brook and Jodi, the best sisters a girl could ask for

Published in 2002 by The Rosen Publishing Group, Inc.
29 East 21st Street, New York, NY 10010

First Edition

Library of Congress Cataloging-in-Publication Data

Paige, Joy.
Cool careers without college for people who love to build things / Joy Paige.— 1st ed.
p. cm. — (Cool careers without college)
Includes bibliographical references and index.
ISBN 0-8239-3506-X (library binding)
1. Engineering—Vocational guidance—Juvenile literature. 2. Skilled labor—Vocational guidance—Juvenile literature. 3. Artisans—Juvenile literature. 4. Journey workers—Juvenile literature. I. Title. II. Series.
TA157 .P25 2001

2001004188

Manufactured in the United States of America

CONTENTS

Introduction 7

1 | Plumber 9

2 | Carpenter 20

3 | Sculptor 31

4 | Construction Worker 42

5 | Auto Mechanic 53

6 | Gardener 64

7 | Doll Maker 75

8 | Tool and Die Maker 85

9 | Shoe Industry Worker 96

10 | Electrician 106

11 | Jeweler and Jewelry Repairer 116

12 | Tailor and Dressmaker 127

Glossary 138

Index 141

INTRODUCTION

Finding a career that's right for you can be tough, especially if you have decided not to go on to college. It's important to consider your interests and hobbies when choosing a profession. Some people prefer to work in a field that utilizes their special skills, and for people who love to build things, there are many options available.

If you're like most people, you spend your free time doing things that you enjoy. Maybe you picked up a love of woodworking in shop class, or you're fascinated by the details of gardening. Either way, you picked up this book because you like to construct things. Even if you're just getting into the basics of carpentry, for example, you may find that the other professions explored in this book are extremely tempting.

This book will walk you through the many jobs you can find if you have a knack for, and a love of, building things. Some of these jobs can be difficult to obtain, but the rewards of finding a job you love are priceless. Read on to learn more about the positions available to those who think that building things is their niche.

1

PLUMBER

Plumbers are a commodity everywhere you go. As plumbing is an essential part of our daily lives, people rely on plumbers to make sure that their plumbing systems function properly. Plumbing systems exist in every modern commercial and residential building. And new buildings are being built constantly, which means there

The construction of every new building provides employment opportunities for skilled and experienced plumbers.

will always be work available for an experienced and skilled plumber.

Plumbers are dedicated to keeping the water supply safe. Their motto, "Plumbers protect the health of the nation," says it all. These are only a few reasons this job is so alluring. Plumbers are valued and necessary in every community.

Job Duties

The daily duties of plumbers vary. Some days they install sinks in people's homes. Other days they are called to install pipes in a bathroom or kitchen. And sometimes they even get the chance to install new hot water and steam boilers, which are required to maintain heat in a house.

Plumbers mainly work with the pipes that carry water into and waste out of the home. They may have to cut into walls in order to gain access to the plumbing system and repair or perform maintenance. They also have to cut pipes and join them back together using clamps, screws, bolts, cement, or solder.

Organizational skills are very important to a plumber. Plumbing systems need to be orderly so that the next person who works on the system can easily understand how it was put together. Of course, maintenance is also a big part of the plumber's job.

Whenever a new home or building is erected, plumbers are called in to install the plumbing fixtures and systems. If a kitchen is being built, a plumber will install the sink. If a bathroom is being built, the plumber will install the sink and shower. Wherever there is a need for water in a home, a plumber is the person to turn to for help.

Education and Training

Richard Noble, a plumber for thirty-four years in New Jersey, explains the ways in which one goes about becoming a plumber: "It takes five years of practical experience in the plumbing trade, working under a journeyman [experienced] plumber. After five years, you apply for a state license and then take a test. The test is all about the plumbing code, which specifies what is required by law for the installation of water lines, waste and vent lines, and building structures."

Most plumbers learned the ins and outs of the trade working as a plumber's apprentice, or helper. Apprentices are often required to carry some of the plumber's heavy equipment and perform some of the lesser tasks of the job. But in exchange for their work, they get hands-on experience in the field. Once a helper learns the many different tasks a plumber must be able to do, he or she is able to start out as a full-fledged plumber.

Salary

The average base salary for a plumber with up to two years of experience is $26,000 per year. Salary increases with experience. The average annual salary for a plumber with

A plumber installs a boiler in a private home.

four or more years working in the business is $44,000. The longer a plumber stays in the business, the higher his or her chances are of forming a solid base of customers who call on him or her when they need work done. Salary depends upon workload; a young plumber should be eager to take on as much work as possible.

Pros and Cons

What are the perks of this profession? "There is a lot of gratification and a feeling that you have performed a necessary service for people," says Noble, when asked how he feels about being a plumber. Also, if you like to build things, getting a kitchen or bathroom in working order is a form of building something. By planning ahead and using the proper tools and their knowledge of plumbing, plumbers work to create something that functions.

But there are downsides to being a plumber as well. "It can be very physically draining at times. Sometimes you have to take a 350-pound bathtub up a flight of stairs," says Noble. Plumbers work on their feet; they don't get a lot of time to rest or sit down. If you become a plumber, you'll be required to carry your equipment with you, and many plumbing supplies, such as water heaters and metal pipes, are heavy. Because of this, it is essential for you to

Fun Fact

Thomas Crapper (1836–1910) has often been credited with inventing the toilet. That, however, is a myth. Crapper lived in England and was the operator of a successful plumbing company called Crapper & Company. He held nine patents related to plumbing, but none were for the toilet.

be in good physical condition, able to lift heavy objects, and able to withstand long hours of hard work.

If a plumber is self-employed in this industry, he or she has to make contacts and have business associates to get work. An outgoing personality helps a plumber meet and stay in contact with people who may know about opportunities for work. It can't hurt to have friends in this industry.

If you're the kind of person who enjoys seeing physical proof of a completed task, then this just might be the career for you. Noble says, "The best part is being able to see the end product of your labor, in the form of a new bathroom or kitchen."

FOR MORE INFORMATION

ASSOCIATIONS

American Water Works Association
1401 New York Avenue NW, Suite 640
Washington, DC 20005
(202) 628-8303
Web site: http://www.awwa.org
The AWWA is an international, nonprofit organization whose goal is to use its research to promote healthy and plentiful drinking water.

International Association of Plumbing and Mechanical Officials
20001 E. Walnut Drive South
Walnut, CA 91789-2825
(909) 595-8449
e-mail: iapmo@iapmo.org
Web site: http://www.iapmo.org
IAPMO is an organization that sets codes to provide the safest and most efficient methods of installing plumbing.

The Plumbing Foundation City of New York, Inc.
44 West 28th Street, 12th Floor
New York, NY 10001
(212) 481-9740
Web site: http://www.plumbingfoundation.org
The Plumbing Foundation City of New York is a nonprofit association whose mission is to ensure public health through the enactment and enforcement of safe plumbing codes.

WEB SITES

Find Plumbing

http://www.findplumbing.com

This professional plumbing Web site contains information to answer any questions you may have about plumbing.

PlumbingWeb

http://www.plumbingweb.com

This site houses a wealth of information about plumbing, including links to Web sites, organizations, and publications.

Roto-Rooter

http://www.rotorooter.com/fun_and_games.html

This section of the Roto-Rooter Web site contains fun trivia, games, contests, and a history of plumbing.

theplumber.com

http://www.theplumber.com

This Web site is devoted to helping both the professional plumber and the novice learn more about plumbing. The site contains articles about plumbing, information on the history of plumbing, and links to other helpful sites.

BOOKS

Black & Decker. *The Complete Guide to Home Plumbing*. Minnetonka, MN: Creative Publishing International, 1998.
This book provides all the information you need to complete your own home-plumbing installations and repairs, including how-to information for all plumbing projects.

Boraas, Tracy. *Plumbers*. Mankato, MN: Capstone Press, 1998.
Plumbers is an introduction to the plumbing career. It explains the duties of plumbers, as well as their importance in every community.

Hamilton, Katie, and Gene Hamilton. *Plumbing for Dummies*. Indianapolis, IN: I D G Books Worldwide, 1999.
Beginners will find this book especially helpful because it provides an introduction to plumbing for those who are just starting out. It also contains step-by-step instructions for common repairs.

Massey, Howard C. *Plumber's Handbook*. Carlsbad, CA: Craftsman Book Company, 1998.
To learn more about the plumbing code, as well as important plumbing specifications and standards, look to this book. It provides all the essential information that plumbers need to know.

Rudman, Jack. *Plumber's Helper*. Syosset, NY: National Learning Corporation, 1994.
If you're in need of a guide to help you learn more about plumbing, look no further. This test preparation guide will provide all you need to know.

Woodson, Dodge R. *International and Uniform Plumbing Codes Handbook*. New York: McGraw-Hill Professional Book Group, 2000.
This easy-to-understand guide will help you learn all you need to know about the plumbing code. It includes tips on safety, troubleshooting, and code requirements.

Yardley, Thompson. *Down the Drain: Explore Your Plumbing*. Brookfield, CT: Millbrook Press, Inc., 1994.
This book discusses the basics of home plumbing and includes information about the water supply.

PERIODICALS

Drinking Water & Backflow Prevention
P.O. Box 33209
Northglenn, CO 80234-3339
(888) FOR-DWBP (367-3927)
Web site: http://www.dwbp-online.com
Drinking Water & Backflow Prevention magazine is dedicated to educating the public about possible hazards associated with the water supply.

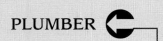

Plumbing and Mechanical
3150 River Road, Suite 101
Des Plaines, IL 60018
Web site: http://www.pmmag.com
This magazine provides information on plumbing, including product reviews, plumbing news, and current plumbing concerns.

VIDEOS

Made Easy: Plumbing **(1986)**
This video provides instructions on performing your own plumbing repairs.

Plumbing **(2000)**
This two-part instructional video won the Home Improvement Video of the Year award by the Librarian Video Review.

2

CARPENTER

If you're the kind of person who likes to use erector sets or Legos to build fantastic creations, you might want to consider a career in carpentry. Carpenters are mainly responsible for building or repairing wood structures for buildings. They do this by reading and following plans and specifications for the buildings they work on.

These are much like blueprints; unless you're trained, they are difficult to read. Carpenters also need to know about things such as a structure's airflow management and insulation techniques.

Job Duties

Carpentry is a division of the construction trade. Carpenters are involved in a variety of different tasks, all related to the construction of buildings. The tasks they are expected to do vary, but generally, carpenters read blueprints to figure out what they will be assembling. Then they cut and measure wood and other materials to fit the specifications in the blueprints. They assemble the materials using nails, glue, and other joining agents. Then they check their work to make sure it has been assembled properly.

So, what do carpenters assemble? Carpenters are called in to install stairs, door frames, hardwood floors, cabinets, and many other things inside the home. They also perform work outside, such as installing exterior trim.

Carpenters who work outside the construction industry have different responsibilities. Sometimes they build furniture. Other times they're called to replace floor tiles or windowpanes. These carpenters have much more freedom in choosing their jobs because they're not limited to helping out with the construction of buildings. For people who

A carpenter and his apprentice install a door for a storage room.

love to build things from wood, this is the ideal situation. As you can see, the job of a carpenter consists of doing many different things.

Education and Training

Getting started in carpentry is much like getting started in plumbing. It's best to do an apprenticeship: Work with a skilled carpenter who can teach you, while also using classroom instruction to learn. (Classroom instruction includes

Carpenters need to take great care when reading plans and taking measurements. Otherwise, they risk wasting time and materials, thereby running up the cost of the job.

lessons in safety, first aid, different carpentry techniques, blueprint reading, mathematics, and sketching.) These two combined methods of learning will ensure that you're well trained and that you learn all of the practical skills you'll need. You can get information on apprenticeship programs by contacting the United Brotherhood of Carpenters and Joiners of America. Certification programs are also offered through some schools, but graduates of those programs usually have to begin as apprentices just like anyone else.

Most carpenters, however, obtain their skills by informal on-the-job training. Working under a skilled carpenter will help you learn all you need to know about the profession. By watching and helping an experienced carpenter, you will pick up the skills that are necessary to perform all of the tasks expected of a person in this profession. Most states require that trained apprentices pass a licensing exam to get permits for jobs. The test is comprised of questions testing applicants' knowledge of carpentry, including safety.

If you think you're interested in pursuing a career in carpentry, you may want to take a class in woodworking first. If such classes are not available in your school, you will surely be able to find one in your area. Check with your local hobby shop for recommendations to a school or center that offers classes. Or consult your local phone book to find community colleges or recreation centers that have classes on woodworking or carpentry.

Salary

According to the *Occupational Outlook Handbook*, salaries for carpenters vary and often depend on the type of carpentry being done. In 1998, the average payment was $14 per hour of work. Considering the opportunities for overtime, you may be able to make a good deal of money in this profession. As a carpenter, your salary will increase with the

Students cut a board on a table saw in a carpentry class.

number of years you practice your trade. More experienced carpenters can earn over $46,000 a year.

Pros and Cons

Carpentry can be a very fulfilling career if you take a lot of pride in your work. Kevin Dowd, a carpenter in Massachusetts, says, "It's great to see what you've built and know it's going to be there for a long time." The things that carpenters build will grace people's homes for years to come. For a carpenter, this knowledge can be quite gratifying.

Did You Know?

One-third of all carpenters are self-employed. This means they work for themselves and don't have to report to a boss. If you're the kind of person who is self-motivated and enjoys having freedom to choose jobs as needed, then carpentry might be ideal for you.

Fun Fact

The motion picture industry (people involved in making movies and shows for television) employs "scenic" carpenters. These people are hired to build sets that will eventually make it onto the big screen!

The job of a carpenter is different almost every day, which means that there is a lot of variation in the work he or she does. Carpenters are never bored at work! There is no need to worry about repetitive job duties.

Carpentry is, however, very physical work. Be prepared to spend a lot of time on your feet. You may be required to carry heavy materials and tools. This profession also requires a lot of time working outside in all kinds of weather. So, if you dislike the outdoors, you might want to consider something else!

Safety is very important in carpentry because carpenters work with tools that, if not handled and used properly, can be very dangerous. People in this profession have to be very focused on the task at hand and always make safety a priority. The risk of danger is lessened by the knowledge of the tools of the trade and following proper safety precautions.

According to the United States Department of Labor, the number of positions available for new carpenters is on the rise. The great need for carpenters, coupled with the ease with which one can learn the job, makes it a very appealing option for many.

FOR MORE INFORMATION

ASSOCIATIONS

Associated General Contractors (AGC) of America
333 John Carlyle Street, Suite 200
Alexandria, VA 22314
(703) 548-3118
Web site: http://www.agc.org
This organization strives to provide information on upcoming industry events. It also provides a magazine, newsletter, videos, and books relating to the construction trades.

Home Builders Institute (HBI)
1090 Vermont Avenue NW, Suite 600
Washington, DC 20005
(202) 371-0600
Web site: http://www.hbi.org
The Home Builders Institute is a part of a larger organization called the National Association of Home Builders. HBI provides education and training, as well as apprenticeship programs for those wanting to learn more about the construction trades.

United Brotherhood of Carpenters and Joiners of America
101 Constitution Avenue NW
Washington, DC 20001
The United Brotherhood of Carpenters and Joiners of America is one of the oldest labor unions.

WEB SITES

Building & Construction Careers—Carpentry
http://www.construction-training.net.au/carpentry.htm
Go to this site to read an interview with a carpenter and find out what it takes to get into this field.

Edunet: Careers—Carpenter
http://www.edunetconnect.com/cat/careers/carpent.html
For more information on whether or not you have what it takes to become a carpenter, visit this site. You'll learn more about what carpenters do and get advice about getting started.

Harcourt Learning Direct—Careers in This Field: Carpenter
http://www.harcourt-learning.com/programs/carpenter/careers.html
This site explains the basics of carpentry, including information on salaries and a group of links to learn even more.

Learn Free.com—Carpentry Tips
http://www.learnfree-home.com/carpentry-g.html

This site provides tips on home carpentry and includes definitions of carpentry terms. You can also search for information on other professions.

Wow Careers—Carpenter—What I Do
http://www.wowcareers.com/careers/carpenter_01.htm
Find out firsthand what it's like to be a carpenter. This Wow Careers site provides information from real professionals.

BOOKS

Abram, Norm. *Measure Twice, Cut Once: Lessons from a Master Carpenter*. New York: Little, Brown & Company, 1995.
People with many different levels of carpentry expertise will enjoy this book. It provides carpentry tips for beginners, as well as checklists for those who are more skilled.

Burby, Liza N., and Diana Star Helmer. *A Day in the Life of a Carpenter*. New York: The Rosen Publishing Group, Inc., 1999.
This book chronicles a day in the life of a carpenter who makes furniture. Check it out to learn more about the duties that are required of a furniture maker.

Wagner, Willis H., and Howard "Bud" Smith. *Modern Carpentry: Building Construction Details in Easy-to-Understand Form*. Tinley Park, IL: Goodheart-Willcox Publisher, 1999.
This book is essential for those just starting out in carpentry. It includes tips on the basics of carpentry, including light construction methods and building material information.

Wallner, Rosemary. *Construction Carpenter*. Mankato, MN: Capstone Press, 2000.
For those interested in becoming a carpenter, this book is ideal. It provides job information, including outlook, educational requirements, skills needed, and more.

PERIODICALS

Fine Woodworking
The Taunton Press, Inc.
63 South Main Street
P.O. Box 5506
Newtown, CT 06470-5506
Web site: http://www.finewoodworking.com
Fine Woodworking is a magazine that specializes in providing information to carpenters, craftspeople, and furniture makers. It includes informative articles to help you learn more about working with wood.

Wood Worker's Journal
P.O. Box 56585
Boulder, CO 80322-6585
Web site: http://www.woodworkersjournal.com
This magazine presents an in-depth look at different woodworking projects and provides step-by-step guides.

VIDEOS

Basic Carpentry Video (1987)
This video will teach you the basics of carpentry tools and how to use them. It is an excellent resource for a beginner.

Fine Woodworking: Mastering Woodworking Machines (1994)
You'll learn about setting up and using your woodworking machinery with this easy-to-understand video.

3

SCULPTOR

Sculptors use different materials to build three-dimensional pieces of art. This job is pursued by those who love art as much as they like building things. Sculptors have a lot of freedom in their jobs and need to keep an eye out for anything that inspires them to create.

Sculpting is something that you can start learning right away.

Art exhibitions such as CowParade, which was displayed in many major cities, make a sculptor's work more accessible to the public.

There is no right or wrong way to build a sculpture, but there are many techniques and tools that you may want to become familiar with when starting a career as a sculptor.

Job Duties

Sculpting is a fine art. It is different from other careers in art, such as graphic design or illustration. Sculptors generally do not work for large corporations, as graphic designers or illustrators may. Sixty percent of sculptors are self-employed, so the work they do is generally for themselves. Their work does not have to conform to an idea given to them by someone else. This allows a lot of job freedom and an ability to produce art that is truly theirs, not influenced by another person or a company.

The exception to this rule is that sculptors may be commissioned and paid to make a piece by a person, group, corporation, or city. Generally, though, this is rare. Sculptors earn money by showing their art in galleries and trying to sell their pieces. Art dealers may also sell sculptures for an artist.

Sculptors may choose from a variety of materials to make their sculptures. Usually, a sculptor uses one material, such as clay, wire, plastic, fabric, glass, metal, or wood. But some sculptors make mixed-media sculptures, which combine many different materials. These works are made by cutting, gluing, sawing, soldering, and molding the material. What's interesting about sculpting is that there are no boundaries within which sculptors must work. Their work is purely creative, and they are allowed the chance to build a sculpture that is ten feet high, if they choose. Mixed-media sculpture allows the sculptor even more room for creativity. Any material he or she chooses

A sculptor carves a swordfish out of a block of ice. Ice sculptors must be able to work quickly and confidently.

can be incorporated. Some artists have even used light and sound to create multisensory experiences that go way beyond just viewing a piece of art.

Education and Training

Getting started in this business can be disappointing because it takes a long time for a sculptor to build a fan base and sell his or her work on a steady basis. It takes a lot of motivation and determination to get recognized.

It takes years of experience to become a skilled sculptor. If you think you might be interested in becoming a sculptor, you'll want to explore the many materials that can be used to sculpt and determine which you most enjoy working with. There are also many techniques that you can utilize once you've learned them. The longer you practice sculpting as a hobby, the more you'll know about the kinds of sculpting that can be done and the kind that you most prefer doing.

Getting a job in this field requires no formal training, although most art schools offer programs where one can learn to sculpt. Becoming a sculptor is more like a hobby or a passion that you can benefit from financially. If you already know how to sculpt and are considering making it your livelihood, try selling some of your art to a gallery or at a craft fair. The more you keep at it, the more likely you will be to sell your pieces. And if you truly love to sculpt, you should consider making it your career.

Most public schools offer art classes as an elective. If you're interested in learning more about sculpting, try taking an art class. You might love it so much that you keep sculpting for the rest of your life.

Salary

Fine artists usually work on a freelance or commission basis. But because of the large quantity of artists trying to

Fun Fact

Norma "Duffy" Lyon is widely known as a sculptor who made life-sized cow sculptures out of butter! Her other creations have included renditions of Elvis Presley, President Dwight D. Eisenhower, and Garth Brooks. Her work paved the way for other sculptors to try new and different materials to work with.

Did You Know?

The culinary industry has a need for food sculptors! Not only is there a demand for people who can carve big

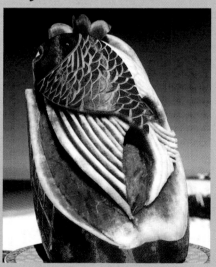

blocks of ice into beautiful creations for parties, but people are also needed to make sculptures out of other foods as well as for presenting food in an attractive manner. The next time you're served a dish with a beautiful flower made from a radish or another vegetable, you'll know it was made by a food sculptor.

Watermelon carved in the shape of a fish

make a living, it's very difficult to exist solely on the money made from selling sculptures. Sculpting is a very competitive field. It's hard to become financially successful as a sculptor. Luckily, there are other opportunities to work in the art industry. Some sculptors find that they can best utilize their skills by working in a museum or art gallery. By doing this, they get to use their skills as artists and still make money to support themselves. Others may teach art classes to other people who want to learn the craft.

Pros and Cons

One of the wonderful things about a career as a sculptor is that, since it is most likely something you truly enjoy doing, you won't mind going to work every day. Keep in mind, though, that it is hard to support yourself when you don't have a steady paycheck. You may go long periods without selling any of your work. Or you may have to pick up a second job to pay your bills. It is, however, very possible to make a good living in this field. You just have to believe in your work and do your best to sell your art.

FOR MORE INFORMATION

ASSOCIATIONS

DeCordova Museum and Sculpture Park
51 Sandy Pond Road
Lincoln, MA 01773-2600
(781) 259-8355
Web site: http://www.decordova.org
This Massachusetts museum and sculpture park offers events and programs related to art and sculpting. The thirty-five-acre sculpture park contains many large, contemporary sculptures, and new works are added often.

International Sculpture Center
14 Fairgrounds Road, Suite B
Hamilton, NJ 08619-3447
(609) 689-1051
e-mail: isc@sculpture.org
Web site: http://www.sculpture.org
The International Sculpture Center is an organization that exists to educate the public about sculpture and help advance the careers of sculptors worldwide.

Sculptor's Society of Canada
P.O. Box 40
2 First Canadian Place, Exchange Tower
130 King Street W.
Toronto, ON M5X 1B5
(416) 214-0389
e-mail: sculpcan@eol.ca
Web site: http://www.sculptures-canada.com

The SSC is dedicated to helping young sculptors and educating the public about the fine art of sculpting.

The Sculpture Center
1834 E. 123rd Street
Cleveland, OH 44106
(216) 229-6527
Web site: http://www.sculpturecenter.org
This nonprofit organization specializes in preserving outdoor sculpture and helping new sculptors get their careers off the ground by allowing them to exhibit their art at the center.

World Sand Sculptors Association
340 Rancheros Drive, Suite 192
San Marcos, CA 92069
e-mail: gkkirk@sandworld.com
Web site: http://www.sandworld.com
The World Sand Sculptors Association is a worldwide organization that holds events and competitions for sand sculpting.

WEB SITES

ArtLex Art Dictionary
http://www.artlex.com
Go to this site to find definitions of over 3,300 art-related terms. It also includes a section of art-related links to learn more.

International Directory of Sculpture Parks and Gardens
http://www.artnut.com/intl.html
This site is devoted to educating those interested in sculpture about the sculpture parks and gardens throughout the world. You can search for sculpture parks and gardens, and obtain reviews and information.

Sculptor.org
http://www.sculptor.org
This site provides resources to sculptors and to people who would like to become sculptors.

BOOKS

Burby, Liza N. *A Day in the Life of a Sculptor*. New York: The Rosen Publishing Group, 1999.
This book shows how a sculpture is made by showing the steps the artist takes to build a metal seahorse.

Erdmann, Dottie. *Hands on Sculpting*. San Diego: Columbine Communications and Publications, 1992.
If you are learning to sculpt, check out this book to learn more about sculpting techniques, materials, and projects. Many pictures and instructions make this book ideal for beginners.

LaFosse, Michael. *Paper Art: The Art of Sculpting with Paper*. Gloucester, MA: Rockport Publishers, 1998.
Learn a new kind of sculpture: paper art! This book introduces the reader to many different uses for paper in sculpture, including paper folding and papier-mâché.

Nigrosh, Leon I. *Sculpting Clay*. Worcester, MA: Davis Publications, Incorporated, 1991.
Learn more about sculpting with clay with this instructional book. Pictures and explanations will help you learn how to make clay figures.

Pekarik, Andrew. *Sculpture*. New York: Hyperion Books for Children, 1992.
This guide to sculpting is easy to read and explains the basics of sculpting concepts.

Plowman, John. *Start Sculpting*. Edison, NJ: Book Sales, Incorporated, 1995.
This book provides instructions for twenty sculpting projects that use easy-to-find materials. For those wanting to jump right into a sculpting project, this book will be useful.

Rich, Jack C. *Materials & Methods of Sculpture*. Mineola, NY: Dover Publications, Incorporated, 1998.
This manual provides clear and concise information on sculpting with many different kinds of materials.

PERIODICALS

Sculpture
1529 18th Street NW
Washington, DC 20036
(202) 234-0555
e-mail: sculpt@dgsys.com
This magazine focuses on the art of sculpting, bringing you all different kinds of information about sculpture.

VIDEOS

I'm All Clay, You're All Clay
This video caters to beginners who want to learn pottery. It covers all the essentials you will need to begin your fun with clay.

Sculpture Classroom (1990)
In this video, Arlene Siegal instructs both beginners and the advanced on how to sculpt.

4

CONSTRUCTION WORKER

According to the U.S. Department of Labor, construction was one of the largest industries in 1998. And it will continue to grow as more buildings go up and others need maintenance. This is not surprising if you consider the many different types of structures that construction workers build and repair. The buildings we live, work, or go to school in, the roads we drive on, and the bridges we ride over were built by and are maintained by construction workers. There will always be a need for people to build structures, and these structures will need to be maintained. This means that there are many jobs available in the field. The availability of work, coupled with a relatively high pay rate, makes construction a very promising field to get into.

Job Duties

The construction industry is divided into three parts. General building contractors are responsible for building things such as houses, schools, stores, and office buildings. Heavy construction contractors build roads, tunnels, sewers, and other "heavy" projects. Special trade contractors are people who specialize in one area of construction but are not responsible for the building as a whole. Plumbers, electricians, and carpenters are all special trade contractors, and their duties are discussed in other chapters throughout this book.

Contractors are people who oversee the building of a structure and hire people to perform different tasks. These people tend to be skilled and experienced construction workers. Their years in the business have given them the knowledge they need to manage the overall construction process. As a contractor, you'll need to know what duties

Construction workers move cautiously as they work on the frame of a building. They know that a misstep may cause them to fall and could lead to injury or even death.

need to be performed before a structure can be completed and hire the appropriate people to do different jobs.

As a construction worker, your job duties will vary, depending on which part of the construction industry you decide to get involved in. If you feel that your interests lie in the building of residential structures, you should try your hand as a house builder and work your way up to general building contractor. Or maybe you've seen a road being built and thought it was fascinating. If so, you may want to consider work on highway or street construction. Then you can work your way up to become a heavy construction contractor. Either way, you would be helping to erect a structure that will stand for many years.

Education and Training

Like many of the professions described in this book, construction workers often start their careers as apprentices, studying and learning under a skilled worker. The apprentice learns the job by watching his or her mentor, and in return, he or she is expected to help out with small tasks. Those who start out as assistants to skilled construction workers perform some of the heavy lifting and cleaning up. It's not glamorous, but it is necessary to learn the craft.

An alternative is enrolling in a formal apprenticeship program, which includes on-the-job training and some classroom training. Apprenticeship programs are available through specialty schools and colleges. No matter which route you choose, you'll start slowly, learning how to use simple machinery. You will learn the craft by watching and experiencing the work yourself.

Salary

Because there are so many different professions that exist in this field, salaries for construction workers vary greatly.

Pros and Cons

One of the benefits of becoming a construction worker is that you'll be able to use your skills wherever you go. The construction industry exists in every state, in every town in the United States and Canada, and beyond. Not only will you have the advantage of job security, but you'll also be paid well for your hard work. Since construction workers are mainly self-employed, you also may have a great boss: yourself! Many people only wish they had the freedom to choose when—and on what jobs—they work. Luckily, for those in this industry, there are many perks.

The downside to being a construction worker is the strenuous physical work. Building big structures requires carrying large, and sometimes heavy, equipment and materials. Construction workers must be physically fit, since their work requires heavy lifting and carrying. In addition to being strong, they have to have stamina, or the ability to perform physically demanding tasks for a long period of time.

Do you like the outdoors? Many construction jobs require workers to perform their duties outside, especially if the job involves the construction of a road or bridge. In the sweltering

Construction work is often taxing, dirty, and dangerous, but builders take great pride in being involved in the creation of a new structure.

Did You Know?

According to the Bureau of Labor Statistics, 10 percent of all workers in the construction industry are female. Within this field, 886,000 workers are women. The National Association of Women in Construction (NAWIC) was founded in 1953 by a group of sixteen female construction workers. Their membership has risen to 6,000, and they have chapters all over the United States and in parts of Canada. So, if you think that construction work is reserved for men, think again!

Fun Fact

The Empire State Building stands 1,454 feet tall. When it was built in 1931, there were 3,000 construction men working at once! The building, which is one of the world's tallest and often referred to as the eighth wonder of the world, is composed of approximately 10,000 bricks. It took seven million man-hours to build!

heat of summer or the extreme cold of winter, these may not be the most appealing work conditions.

Another downside to working in the construction industry is that it can be dangerous. Many of the tools that are used to build things can be harmful if used incorrectly or if there is an accident. Injured construction workers often are forced to find a new way to make a living. This is why it's so important to be properly trained.

The things that are built by construction workers stand for a very long time. People rely on construction workers to build them comfortable homes, safe roads and bridges, and strong buildings that will be admired and used for years to come.

FOR MORE INFORMATION

ASSOCIATIONS
Associated Builders and Contractors
1300 North 17th Street, Suite 800
Rosslyn, VA 22209
(703) 812-2000
Web site: http://www.abc.org
Associated Builders and Contractors is a national trade organization that focuses on ensuring top-of-the-line craftsmanship. The association

COOL CAREERS WITHOUT COLLEGE

has chapters across the country and offers safety programs to members of the organization.

National Association of Home Builders
1201 15th Street NW
Washington, DC 20005
(800) 368-5242
Web site: http://www.nahb.com
This organization's main goal is to ensure that safe buildings are built and that affordable housing is available to everyone.

WEB SITES

Job Guide 2001—Construction Worker
http://jobguide.thegoodguides.com.au/text/jobdetails.cfm?jobid=1101
This site will give you the specifics of the work of a construction worker, including tasks, related careers, and personal requirements.

Salvadori Center: Education and the Built Environment
http://www.salvadori.org
Check out this site to learn more about different structures, how they are built, and what materials are used to make them.

BOOKS

Liebing, Ralph. *Introduction to the Construction Industry*. Upper Saddle River, NJ: Prentice Hall, 2000.
This book explains how the construction industry works. It provides important construction industry terminology, as well as details of the steps taken to complete a construction project.

Moore, Caire. *Concrete Form Construction*. Albany, NY: Delmar Publishers, 1994.
This book provides information on concrete form construction. It is ideal for those looking to learn more about the uses of concrete in construction.

Pasternak, Ceel. *In Construction*. Manassas Park, VA: Impact Publications, 2000.

This book showcases the work of many female construction workers. It also provides details on getting started and flourishing as a female in this male-dominated industry.

Salvadori, Mario G. *The Art of Construction: Projects and Principles for Beginning Engineers and Architects*. Chicago: Chicago Review Press, 1990. This book explains the basic principles of building large architectural structures, such as bridges and skyscrapers.

Stone, Tanya Lee. *Construction Wonders*. Woodbridge, CT: Blackbirch Press, Incorporated, 1998.
Learn more about ten of the most incredible construction wonders. Details of such amazing structures such as the Sears Tower and the Alaska pipeline are discussed in this book.

Walker, Lester R. *Housebuilding for Children*. New York: Overlook Press, 1990.
Younger readers with an interest in building homes will especially enjoy this book. It provides practice projects and information on tools to help the reader learn more.

PERIODICALS

Building Design & Construction
1350 E. Touhy Avenue
Des Plaines, IL 60018
Web site: http://www.bdcmag.com
This magazine aims to educate the reader about many different aspects of construction and building design. It includes news, tips, and information on upcoming events.

International Construction
9800 Metcalf Avenue
Overland Park, KS 66212
(913) 341-1300
Web site: http://intlconstruction.com
International Construction contains information on construction, including industry news, information on equipment, and feature articles.

VIDEOS

House Construction Ahead (1995)
This video explains all aspects of house construction in an easy-to-understand way. It includes footage of actual construction work to help explain how it's done.

Mighty Construction Machines
The host of this video takes the audience to actual construction sites to learn more about construction. Interviews with construction workers and explanations of the big machines used for construction help the viewer to learn more.

Road Construction Ahead (1991)
This video focuses on the construction of roads. You'll see the construction of a road and the many steps that are taken to build one.

5

AUTO MECHANIC

Do you have an interest in cars? Maybe you spend your free time watching race-car driving on television or collecting miniatures of hot rods of the past. Maybe you've even begun to fix up your own car. Auto mechanics doesn't have to remain just a hobby. Many people make a living fixing cars. In fact, there were 790,000 people working as automotive mechanics and service technicians in the United States in 1998. Like many of the careers in this book, auto mechanics are needed everywhere. In addition, the U.S. Department of Labor reports that opportunities are expected to increase in this industry in the future.

Job Duties

Auto mechanics provide a necessary service to anyone who owns a car. From time to time, every car needs work, whether it requires new brakes or a routine oil change. Mechanics inspect, maintain, and repair cars that are brought in for work. In order to fix a car that is not running properly, a mechanic first has to diagnose the problem, much like a doctor would for a patient. He or she asks the car's owner about any "symptoms" the car has shown. Using the information the owner gives to the mechanic, the mechanic goes through the proper steps, usually using special tools and diagnostic equipment, to figure out what needs to be repaired.

A customer pays close attention to her mechanic as he checks her car. Automobile owners prefer mechanics who listen and explain, in simple terms, what's wrong and what needs to be done.

Routine service for a car works much differently. Usually, the mechanic has a checklist of things to look for when servicing automobiles. He or she goes down the list, inspecting the car and its parts, ensuring that the car is in proper working order and fixing the things that aren't.

Automotive technology is becoming more and more complex. These days, new cars are run largely by computers (in fact, the first spaceship had fewer computers than a car does today!). This means that automotive mechanics work with these computer systems, not just nuts and bolts. In this increasingly computer-driven industry, auto mechanics face the difficulty of learning and using these new systems. In fact, mechanics who have the skills to repair these complex systems are often called service technicians.

Education and Training

Getting started in the automotive repair industry isn't as easy as you might think. It takes more than a love of cars to become a mechanic. For starters, aptitude in math, electronics, and computers helps. These are skills you'll need to use on the more complex car systems, which require the mechanic to work with new, sophisticated technologies.

For this reason, it is almost always necessary to enroll in a training program. Some high schools offer these programs,

Service technicians check a car's computer system.

but depending on the school, you may not be taught the newest technologies. Most community colleges and technical schools do offer the kind of programs that will teach you all you need to know to start your auto mechanic career. In these programs, classroom training is combined with actual repair work to give you a complete understanding of the inner workings of a car and how to fix one, even the most technologically complex.

A training program is valuable because as an auto mechanic, you'll be expected to diagnose a car problem very quickly. People who have car problems don't want to leave the shop with a car that is still in disrepair. Cars contain so many complex systems, and auto mechanics must have a great deal of knowledge about each one. As the technology gets more and complex, it's necessary to understand not just the mechanical parts of a car but also the electrical systems.

Salary

Auto mechanics are usually paid well. In 1998, the average hourly wage for auto mechanics was $13. The highest 10 percent of people in this field earned $21 per hour. There may be opportunities for overtime, too.

Pros and Cons

If you're a person who loves to work on cars, then being an auto mechanic would allow you to make a living doing something you enjoy. You'd be able to practice your hobby and get paid for it! Also, employers tend to send their workers to learn the newest methods for auto repair, so you would also be learning more about what you love.

One of the drawbacks of this job may be your work environment. Some repair shops can be dirty and poorly lit. Also, there may be tools and parts lying around, which

A mechanic works under a car—not the most comfortable position to be in for an extended period of time.

invites injuries. The noise of the machines may bother you, and if the shop is drafty, you may be cold during the winter. But keep in mind that most automotive repair shops are kept clean and are safe. It's up to you to choose a workplace that you're comfortable in. Another drawback is that you'll be expected to lift heavy parts and remain in uncomfortable positions for extended periods of time. For those who don't have the physical strength or stamina, this could be a problem.

Other Options

If you're interested in becoming an auto mechanic, you may want to consider other similar professions. If your interest in mechanics isn't strictly limited to auto-mobiles, why don't you look into a career as a motor-cycle, boat, aircraft, or small-engine mechanic? Or maybe your interest lies only with a career working with cars. If that is the case, you may want to look into a career as an automotive body repairer or a repair service estimator.

Automotive body repairers are responsible for fixing

any dents or problems with the outside of a car. They are the people who make the exterior of a car look like new after an acci-dent. A repair service estimator checks an automobile and deter-mines the need for repairs then estimates the cost of repairs.

An aircraft mechanic works on the large engine of a plane.

FOR MORE INFORMATION

ASSOCIATIONS

Automotive Service Association, Inc.
P.O. Box 929
Bedford, TX 76095-0929
(817) 283-6205
(800) 272-7467
e-mail: asainfo@asashop.org
Web site: http://www.asashop.org
The Automotive Service Association is a fifty-year-old organization with over 12,000 members. The goal of the ASA is to promote education and knowledge of car mechanics by making resources available to its members.

Women's Automotive Association International
6050 Tomken Road
Mississauga, ON L5T 1X8
(888) 335-3930
e-mail: waai@mf.com
Web site: http://www.waai.com
This organization focuses on women and their role in the automotive industry. It supports women in the automotive industry by offering support, information, and scholarships to women with an interest in an automotive-related career.

WEB SITES

The Art of Automotive Repair
http://www.sjmautotechnik.com/repair.html
This site is a valuable resource if you have questions about how to fix an automobile or need help troubleshooting a car that's not functioning properly. It has information on tools, symptoms, and environmental effects on a car.

Auto Mechanic—Occupational Guides
http://www.labor.state.ny.us/html/guides/automech.htm
This Web site provides information on auto mechanics, including job duties, job outlook, and the requirements needed to get into this field. It also includes links to find out more about becoming an auto mechanic.

Automotive Technology Career Information
http://www.wcc.cc.il.us/careers/automotive.html
This site will help you figure out if you're cut out to work with automobiles. It has information on the different careers available in this field, as well as lists of typical equipment, necessary skills, and salary ranges.

Carcrisis Online
http://www.carcrisis.com
This is the online version of the newspaper column "Carcrisis." It helps to explain common car problems and the way to go about fixing them.

BOOKS

Boraas, Tracey. *Auto Mechanics*. Mankato, MN: Capstone Press, 1998. This book describes the duties of an auto mechanic and provides information on tools, places of employment, and uniforms.

Harrison, William C. *Here Is Your Career: Auto Mechanic*. New York: The Putnam Publishing Group, 1997. This easy-to-understand book will help you learn more about a career in auto mechanics.

Hathaway, Richard B., and John Robert Lindbeck. *Complete Auto Mechanics*. New York: Macmillan Publishing Company, Incorporated, 1991.

Learn all you need to know about auto mechanics! If you're interested in fixing cars as a career or hobby, this book provides information about car repair.

Rudman, Jack. *Auto Mechanics.* Syosset, NY: National Learning Corporation, 1997.
This guide provides help in passing automotive repair tests. It is helpful for those looking into a career as an auto mechanic.

PERIODICALS

Car and Driver
2002 Hogback Road
Ann Arbor, MI 48105
(734) 971-3600
e-mail: editors@caranddriver.com
Web site: http://www.caranddriver.com
Car and Driver presents reviews of automobiles, articles about automobiles, and industry news.

Popular Mechanics
810 Seventh Avenue
New York, NY 10019
(212) 649-2000
e-mail: popularmechanics@hearst.com
Web site: http://www.popularmechanics.com
Popular Mechanics is a magazine that focuses on current news about cars and car technology. Among other things, its editors include information about new cars, car technology, car care, and motorsports.

VIDEOS

How a Car Is Built (1995)
Think Media
This video shows a car being built from beginning to end. It shows how sheet metal is used in the very first stages of building a car and all the steps that must be taken before a car is ready for the road.

6

GARDENER

The term "gardener" can be used to describe a variety of occupations that allow one to work on maintaining lawns, flower beds, trees, and other flora. These jobs can be very fulfilling if you have an interest in planting and shaping gardens or lawns. In addition, the work you put into building a garden or maintaining a piece of land will result in something beautiful, something that will be admired and praised by others.

Job Duties

If you're considering a career in this field, you have many options. Greenhouse workers care for and grow plants in a greenhouse so that they can later be planted. They nurture the seeds for the plants they want to grow and care for the seeds until they're ready to be put into the ground. This job will allow you to learn about many different types of plants and will give you the freedom to experiment with different growing techniques.

Landscape laborers are required to install the plants and trees into the ground. They usually follow a predetermined plan for planting a garden. Landscape laborers are expected to safely transport plants from the greenhouse and install them, then care for them and make sure they are healthy and attractive. They need to have an eye for which flowers and plants look best where, but they also must have knowledge about the conditions under which different plants thrive. Landscape laborers may do their work for private residences and corporate buildings, on estates, and in cities and parks.

Lawn service workers care for lawns. They may be responsible for cleaning up the lawn of a private residence or a commercial area, such as a mall. They mow lawns, trim

A greenhouse gardener puts a lot of hard work into tending his or her plants.

shrubbery, inspect the lawns for problems, and make sure lawns are growing well.

Gardening is an art in itself; many gardeners look at the soil as an artist would see a blank canvas. Much planning and preparation is needed, and the best gardeners are the most experienced.

Education and Training

If you've already begun planting a garden, or if you enjoy mowing or taking care of the lawn, you're on the right track.

An interest in flora is also helpful, since you will be working with plants, flowers, and trees daily. But how do you get involved in this industry?

Entry-level positions usually don't require formal education. You will learn all you need to know by on-the-job training. You must be willing to learn duties of the job and show enthusiasm in order to get ahead. It's also essential that you're able to follow directions. Your supervisor will teach you how to do your job, but you have to be open to learning.

If you're going to be working with pesticides (chemicals that are used to kill unwanted "pests" that destroy plants), most states will require you to pass a test. They will test you on your knowledge of using, and disposing properly of, pesticides. It's a precautionary procedure that is used to ensure that no person is harmed by these toxic chemicals.

There are many schools and organizations that offer gardening classes for people of all ages and levels of skill. The Brooklyn Botanic Garden offers classes such as Earth Movers, for thirteen- to seventeen-year-olds, and Discovery Programs to learn more about plant life. Check your local phone book for schools in your area that offer these kinds of classes.

You can start right now by learning all you can about gardening and putting your new knowledge to practice. You can plant a garden in your backyard, or if space is limited, you can even plant flowers in a flowerpot on your windowsill. The possibilities are endless!

Salary

Entry-level labor positions usually pay minimum wage, but as gardeners gather experience, their salaries increase. The average wage for landscape laborers was $8 an hour in 1998. With more experience, higher paying managerial positions are obtainable. Greenhouse managers and lawn service managers made an average of $12 per hour in 1998.

Pros and Cons

If you already have an interest in gardening, an occupation in this industry would allow you to practice what you love. And the longer you stay in a gardening profession, the more you will learn. Being able to work at a job that you truly enjoy is a wonderful thing.

Jobs in this industry are plentiful and available all over the country. Wherever there are lawns that need mowing, or flowers that need to be planted, there are opportunities to get work.

One of the downsides of this industry is that there isn't much work during the winter months. Opportunities abound when plants are flourishing, but in the cold of winter, most plants don't grow. That means you'll either have to find temporary employment during the "dry spells," head to warmer climates, or make sure you've worked enough during the nice weather to make sufficient money to carry you through the winter.

Gardening is hard work. The work is usually outdoors, sometimes in very warm weather. Also, this work requires a lot of physical exertion. It is not uncommon to be expected to bend down often and carry heavy equipment. But it is a small price to pay for a career that you love.

Did You Know?

Plants need water to grow, right? But did you know that there are some plants, called aquatic plants, that live completely under water? Plants usually get the carbon dioxide they need from the air. So how do aquatic plants thrive under water? These plants don't need air to live because they get the oxygen and food they need from the surrounding water and from photosynthesis, which is the act of turning water, carbon dioxide, and sunlight into carbohydrates and oxygen. The people who care for these plants are called aquatic gardeners. To find out more about aquatic gardening, visit the Aquatic Gardeners Association online: http://www.aquatic-gardeners.org.

Fun Fact

You may think that soil is an essential part of gardening. But that's not necessarily true! Hydroponic gardening is the act of growing plants without using soil. Experts claim that plants grown hydroponically will grow 30 to 50 percent more quickly. So how is it done? Hydroponic gardening requires no soil, but instead, water and nutrients are delivered to the plant. These extra nutrients help the plant to flourish. The lack of soil ensures fewer diseases and fewer bugs. This method of gardening has been called the wave of the future.

A hydroponic farm

FOR MORE INFORMATION

ASSOCIATIONS

National Park Foundation
P.O. Box 57473
Washington, DC 20037
(202) 785-4500
Web site: http://www.nationalparks.org
This nonprofit organization is dedicated to preserving national parks and keeping them safe and attractive. The Web site includes a section about job opportunities. Check it out!

Professional Grounds Management Society
720 Light Street
Baltimore, MD 21230
(800) 609-7467
Web site: http://www.pgms.org
This organization provides information on professional grounds management, with a focus on environmental awareness and keeping the earth healthy and safe.

WEB SITES

Gardening.com
http://www.gardening.com
This online magazine contains information on many different aspects of gardening. You'll learn different methods of growing plants and flowers, and get tips on improving your garden. You can even sign up for a free gardening.com newsletter.

Gardening for Kids Theme Page
http://www.cln.org/themes/gardening.html
This Web site has fun tips and projects for kids to learn more about gardening. It includes tips for starting your own garden and links to other sites to learn even more.

Gardenseeker
http://www.gardenseeker.com
This online database contains lots of information on gardening, including an online magazine with tips and articles relating to gardening.

BOOKS

Davis, Becke, Daria Price Bowman, and Harriet Cramer. *Garden Blueprints: 25 Easy-to-Follow Designs for Beautiful Landscapes*. London: Metro Books, 2000.
Gardeners looking to build a garden will find plans, instructions, and ideas for creating designs for their gardens in this book.

Freeman, Mark. *Building Your Own Greenhouse*. Mechanicsburg, PA: Stackpole Books, 1997.
This book provides instructions and information about building a greenhouse. It also features examples of different greenhouse structures.

Nash, Helen. *Plants for Water Gardens: The Complete Guide to Aquatic Plants*. New York: Sterling Publishing Company, Incorporated, 1999.
This detailed manual provides information on aquatic plants and water gardens. It includes directions for choosing and caring for aquatic plants.

Sanders, Kay, and Mary Helen Schiltz. *Better Homes and Gardens Home Landscaping: Plants, Projects, and Ideas for Your Yard*. Des Moines, IA: Meredith Books, 1996.
If you're looking for instructions and ideas for your own home garden, look no further. This book provides tips and detailed information regarding home landscaping.

Van Hazinga, Cynthia. *Flower Gardening Secrets: Sensible Advice from Seasoned Gardeners*. Alexandria, VA: Time-Life, Incorporated, 1997. The gardening enthusiast will enjoy the tips and advice this book offers on home gardening.

PERIODICALS

Better Homes and Gardens
P.O. Box 37429
Boone, IA 50037-0429
Web site: http://www.bhg.com
This is a monthly publication dedicated to the improvement of your home and garden. It includes pictures and guides to helpful projects to beautify and improve your home.

Fine Gardening
The Taunton Press, Inc.
63 South Main Street
Newtown, CT 06470
Web site: http://www.taunton.com/fg
Fine Gardening is a magazine for people who love gardening. It includes tips on improving your garden, as well as information to help you improve your gardening knowledge.

Flower & Garden
(800) 878-7855
Web site: http://www.flowerandgardenmag.com
If you need information or advice about growing your own garden or flowers, this magazine provides tips and articles that can help you.

Growing Edge
P.O. Box 1027
Corvallis, OR 97339-1027
Web site: http://www.growingedge.com
This magazine focuses on the different methods of growing things, such as hydroponics. It includes articles that focus on the newest and best ways to cultivate your garden.

VIDEOS

Container Gardening from the Ground Up (1997)
If you don't have a lot of space to start a garden, this tape will teach you all you need to know to start a container garden.

How to Grow Plants in a Greenhouse
This video focuses on greenhouse growing techniques. It is ideal for those whose main interest is greenhouse growing.

7

DOLL MAKER

Do you love dolls? Are you a person who collects dolls or has a dollhouse? Have you ever considered making a doll of your own? Many people are fascinated by the different types of dolls that exist. They seek out new and interesting dolls for their collections. The dolls you see in every major toy store are probably made in a factory, but that doesn't mean they're the only ones out there. Handmade dolls are sought out by collectors and doll enthusiasts everywhere.

The art of doll making is complex and involves many intricate steps. While it's a hobby for some people, others choose to make it their career. If you love dolls, you could earn a living from building dolls for others to enjoy.

Job Duties

The job duties of a doll maker vary greatly depending on the type of doll that he or she builds. There are many different types of dolls, each made with different materials, constructed to be a variety of sizes. Considering the type of doll you like best will help you figure out what kind of dolls you would like to make.

Porcelain dolls, for example, are very popular. They are made using molds. First, a doll maker creates the doll's head by pouring liquid clay into a mold. Then the mold is put into a kiln, which is an oven for drying ceramics. In the kiln, the clay becomes porcelain. This porcelain head is the center around which the doll will be built. Once the head cools, a face must be painted on; artistic ability is a must. A wig is added to the head to give the doll hair and a body is constructed of various materials, such as cotton, bendable wire, and cloth. Finally, the doll is dressed. A doll maker has

A doll maker paints the lips of a new doll.

a lot of freedom in choosing the dress for his or her creation. If you love fashion or sewing, making clothes for your dolls will be a lot of fun.

Cloth dolls are also very popular but require different skills to build. First the doll maker must choose a pattern for the cloth doll he or she wants to create. A pattern bought from a store or one made by the doll maker can be used. Once the pattern has been chosen, the doll maker must choose the material he or she wants to use. The material is then sewn together, stuffed with cotton, wool, or another

Students sew tartan clothing for dolls.

kind of doll stuffing, and then decorated. Facial features may be added, as well as clothing, hair, and footwear.

Education and Training

The best way to get started as a doll maker is to make it your hobby. You can begin right away. There are kits available at craft stores that can help you begin. Porcelain doll kits usually contain ready-made doll parts to make construction easier. Once you've become more experienced, you will probably want to learn how to make these parts yourself.

Luckily, there are workshops and classes available every-where that will teach you how to do this yourself. In fact, there are over 700 workshops throughout the world devoted to porcelain doll making.

Craft stores also often carry fabric, patterns, and other materials to start your own cloth doll. You can even find spare doll parts to make your first doll easier to build. You may want to learn to sew if you're interested in making cloth dolls. Sewing is a skill that will surely come in handy for doll makers.

There are many books that can help you get started, no matter what kind of doll making you're interested in. Keep in mind that practice makes perfect. The more dolls you make, the better you will become at making them. So, if your first doll isn't as perfect as you'd like it to be, keep up the hard work and try again!

Salary

As with other kinds of art, doll making does not guarantee a high salary. Doll makers have to work hard at selling their dolls. This may mean working weekends at crafts fairs or setting up their own Web sites to display pictures of their creations and selling them online. No matter how a doll maker chooses to sell his or her dolls, the business side of this vocation is almost another job in itself.

Pros and Cons

The job of a doll maker is much like other artistic jobs. One of the best things about being a doll maker is having complete control over your work environment and the hours that you work.

The salary of a doll maker depends on how many dolls one can sell and how much each doll costs. As with other artistic jobs, you may have to pick up a second job to support yourself until you're able to live solely on what you earn as a doll maker. If you're interested in sharing your knowledge of doll making, you can teach a workshop or give private lessons to make some extra money while working in the field that you love.

Did You Know?

Doll collecting is a very popular hobby. People around the world collect many different kinds of dolls, such as Barbie dolls, ethnic dolls, and antique dolls. Dolls in perfect condition can be worth several thousand dollars. A doll appraiser is a person who specializes in appraising the worth of a doll and is able to tell you how much your dolls are worth.

Fun Fact

Raggedy Ann and Andy, possibly the most famous rag dolls in history, were originally conceived by Johnny Gruelle, an illustrator and comic strip writer. His creations weren't just dolls, though. Raggedy Ann and Andy were the characters in *Raggedy Ann Stories* and *Raggedy Andy Stories*, children's books published in 1918 and 1920. The books may not be remembered by all, but Gruelle's rag doll creations sure are!

Raggedy Ann and Andy dolls

FOR MORE INFORMATION

ASSOCIATIONS

The Academy of American Doll Artists
73 North Spring Street
Concord, NH 03301
(603) 226-4501
e-mail: joyce@aadadoll.org
Web site: http://www.aadadoll.org
This organization is composed of doll makers from around the globe. The aim of the Academy of American Doll Artists is to ensure that doll makers have the opportunity to sell their crafts and be in touch with others who share their love of doll making.

International Foundation of Doll Makers
1941 Geysor Trace
Lawrenceville, GA 30044
(770) 609-3177
e-mail: ifdmgeorgia@hotmail.com
Web site: http://www.ifdm.org
The IFDM is an organization that offers classes and workshops to learn more about doll making. Its magazine, *Doll Makers Workshop*, helps to educate the reader about doll making by providing tips and helpful information on antique reproduction and modern doll making.

WEB SITES

The Doll Mall
http://www.thedollmall.com
This Web site is a resource for artists to learn more about doll making and to get in touch with other doll makers. It contains a gallery of artists' work and hints and tips for doll making.

VirtualDOLLS

http://www.virtualdolls.com

This Web site is an online community of doll collectors. Articles, bulletin boards, and chat rooms connect doll collectors all over the world to share news and information about doll collecting.

BOOKS

Anderson, Debra, and Peter Bell. *Porcelain Doll Making*. Livonia, MI: Scott Publications, 1997.
For those interested in learning porcelain doll making, this book will provide more information to start your hobby or career.

Mahren, Sue. *Make Your Own Teddy Bears and Bear Clothes*. Charlotte, VT: Williamson Publishing Company, 2000.
Beginners will learn the basics of building a teddy bear and teddy bear clothing with this book. It provides instructions and patterns to build your own doll.

Merritt, Alicia. *Book of Dollmaking*. Edison, NJ: Book Sales, Incorporated, 1998.
This book will help both the beginner and the seasoned doll maker. It includes tips and techniques for making different kinds of dolls.

Peake, Pamela. *The Complete Book of Dollmaking: A Practical Step-by-Step Guide to More Than 50 Traditional and Contemporary Techniques*. New York: Watson-Guptill Publications, Incorporated, 1997.
You'll learn about the many different materials and techniques that are used in doll making. Subjects range from making molds to pattern cutting, and more.

Piper, Eloise. *Sewing & Sculpting Dolls: Easy-to-Make Dolls from Fabric, Modeling Paste and Polymer Clay*. Iola, WI: Krause Publications, 1997.
The instructions for doll making in this book are broken down into easy-to-understand steps, which lead you through the doll-making process from beginning to end.

Ryan, Kathleen. *Doll Artists at Work*. Davie, FL: Infodial, 1995.
This book explores the work of many well-known doll artists. You'll get a glimpse into the lives of people who have made a name for themselves making dolls.

PERIODICALS

The Cloth Doll
P.O. Box 2167
Dept. CD-O
Lake Oswego, OR 97035-0051
e-mail: TheClothDoll@TheClothDoll.com
Web site: http://theclothdoll.com
This magazine caters to the cloth doll maker who wants to learn more about his or her craft. Each issue contains free patterns for dolls, featured artists, and information on upcoming doll events.

Dollmaking
N7450 Aanstad Road
P.O. Box 5000
Iola, WI 54945-5000
(800) 331-0038
e-mail: Dollmaking@dollmakingartisan.com
Each issue of *Dollmaking* includes information that doll makers of all levels of experience can enjoy. It has tips and techniques for doll making, as well as news about new products and instructions for fun projects.

Doll World
306 E. Parr Road
Berne, IN 46711
e-mail: Customer_Service@whitebirches.com
Web site: http://www.dollworld-magazine.com
This magazine brings a wealth of information about dolls to the doll enthusiast. In each issue you'll find information about doll collecting, repairing, and history.

8

TOOL AND DIE MAKER

Tools are instruments that are made to perform a specific function. Dies are metal forms that are also made to perform a specific task. The manufacturing of most products requires tools and dies. Tools and dies contribute to the manufacturing process by enabling machines to properly produce a product. Tool and die makers are responsible for making these tools and dies from start to finish. Tools and dies are a necessary part of the manufacturing process because without them, machines would not have the proper accessories to make a product, whether it be something as complex as automotive parts or as simple as an article of clothing.

Job Duties

The job duties of a tool or die maker are very complex. One must be very skilled to complete his or her job. A person may be expected to produce both tools and dies, or may specialize in one or the other. Either way, the job functions the same way and requires the same skills.

Tool and die makers are given an idea of what they will be making, usually by consulting blueprints, plans, drawings, or instructions. They are then responsible for figuring out how they will make the tool or die. They draw up a plan for themselves for how they will go about making the product and then begin. The process involves a lot of precision, so one must be very focused, organized, and driven.

Workers then begin to create their tools or dies. They will need to cut, form, or make a mold to create the pieces that will come together as a finished tool or die. They may have to use other machines to cut any metal they're using. This requires knowledge of many different kinds of machinery. They must also have knowledge of different kinds of metal because they must decide which kind to use. Once the pieces

Did You Know?

The American inventor Eli Whitney changed the face of tool and die making in 1798. The United States government asked him to produce 10,000 muskets, which were weapons used in combat. Whitney discovered that he could design machines to make separate, identical pieces that then could be easily assembled to make a musket. Before this, the pieces were each made by hand. Whitney's discovery shortened the production time and paved the way for modern tool and die making.

are complete, workers put them together to form their tool or die. This process also may include polishing the metal surface or grinding it to make it smooth.

The last step of the process is to ensure that their tools or dies conform to the specifications that were given. They test their products to make sure that they can perform the functions for which they were intended.

As computers become more advanced, tool and die makers increasingly use them to help make their products. When coming up with a plan for how they will make their tools and dies, tool and die makers rely on computers to help calculate measurements and produce accurate drawings of the parts.

This helps ensure the accuracy of the process. Computers help speed up production time and make the job of a tool or die maker easier.

Education and Training

Tool and die makers are highly skilled. You do not need a college education to become a tool or die maker, but the training is intense. It takes four or five years of training before one can practice the trade. A formal apprenticeship program is the best way to get the experience you'll need to start your career as a tool or die maker. Apprenticeship programs combine classroom instruction and practical on-the-job training to give you the best preparation. These programs are rare, though. There aren't many of them, so most tool and die makers acquire their skills through other methods, such as informal on-the-job training or classroom instruction at a vocational school.

When learning to perform the duties of a tool or die maker, you will learn to operate the machines that help make tools and dies. You will also learn all about reading blueprints and plans, and you will learn the many steps involved in tool and die making. Good math skills are essential, as are good eyesight and excellent problem-solving skills.

A worker sits at a die-casting machine, making zinc alloy toys shaped like 1957 Chevys.

Salary

Skilled tool and die makers are few. The lengthy training process is unappealing to a lot of people, so the ones who stick it out are valued. According to the U.S. Department of Labor, the average earnings of a tool and die maker were $37,000 in 1998. And the longer a tool and die maker sticks with the profession, the more he or she is bound to make.

Pros and Cons

Safety is very important in this industry. The use of many dangerous machines has forced factories to take extra precautions. Most machines have protective gear to ensure the safety of the user.

The areas in which tool and die makers work tend to be clean. Also, the rooms are kept cool because the machines need cool air to function properly and to prevent overheating.

It has been estimated that there will be a decline in the number of tool and die makers needed in coming years. Because of the increased use of computers, some of the skills that tool and die makers have will no longer be necessary. Luckily, the skills that are obtained through training can be used in other industries, such as making machinery used in aircraft and automobiles.

Other Options

There are other occupations you may be interested in that are very similar to tool and die making and that require the same skills. Machinists work with machines to produce metal parts used in various products. Much like tool and die makers, they work primarily with machines to build a finished product.

A welder is a person who makes his or her living welding metal. Welding is the act of joining pieces of metal together using heat. Welders are needed in many industries. In the construction industry, welders may weld beams or pipes together. They may also weld parts together when a bridge is built.

A high school junior uses an oxyfuel torch to cut grooves into her metal project.

FOR MORE INFORMATION

ASSOCIATIONS

National Tooling and Machining Association
9300 Livingston Road
Fort Washington, MD 20744
(301) 248-6200
Web site: http://www.ntma.org
This organization contains about 2,600 members and was founded in 1943. It promotes apprenticeship programs and provides managerial workshops to those in the tooling and machining industry.

Precision Metalforming Association
Tool and Die Division
6363 Oak Tree Boulevard
Independence, OH 44131-2500
Web site: http://www.metalforming.com
The Precision Metalforming Association is an organization that serves the metalforming industry. Its magazine, *Metalforming*, contains news, articles, and information on safety to help you learn more about metalworking.

Tooling and Manufacturing Association
1177 South Dee Road
Park Ridge, IL 60068
(847) 825-1120
Web site: http://www.tmanet.com
The Tooling and Manufacturing Association is a nonprofit organization that exists to help people and companies in the tooling and manufacturing industries. The organization also offers courses and training programs.

WEB SITES

GetTech: Tool and Die Maker
http://www.gettech.org/text/html/careers/newman/tool_die.htm
Learn more about tool and die making on this site. There are important facts about trends in this career, as well as the work that is involved.

Metal Web News
http://www.metalwebnews.com
Go here to find out about upcoming metalworking news and events. There is also a discussion group and links to other sites related to metal and metalworking.

Tool and Die Maker
http://www.apprenticesearch.com/fptrades/tool-die.asp
This Web site delivers more information about the job duties of a tool and die maker. It also includes information about apprenticeships and the skills you'll need to get into this field.

BOOKS

Astakhov, Viktor. *Metal Cutting Mechanics*. Boca Raton, FL: CRC Press LLC, 1998.
For those interested in working with metal, this book provides information on metal cutting. Topics such as metal cutting theories, the history of metal cutting, and problem solving are included.

Dudzinski, George A. *Opportunities in Tool and Die Careers*. Lincolnwood, IL: NTC Contemporary Publishing Group, 1993.
This book provides information about the job opportunities available in the tool and die industry.

Fields, Carl L. *Exploring Careers in the Tool and Die Industry*. New York: The Rosen Publishing Group, Inc., 1985.
Career options in the tool and die industry are discussed in this book. It's a must-read for those who want to learn more about a career as a tool and die maker.

COOL CAREERS WITHOUT COLLEGE

Nichols, Jeffrey A. *Getting Started in Metals*. New York: John Wiley & Sons, 1995.
If you're interested in the economics of metals, this book provides expert information about investing in metals.

Thompson, Steve. *Handbook of Mold, Tool, and Die Repair Welding*. Norwich, NY: William Andrew, Incorporated, 1999.
This guide to repairing molds, tools, and dies is an invaluable resource to machinists and welders. It includes tips, techniques, and step-by-step advice on welding.

PERIODICALS

American Tool, Die & Stamping News
42400 Grand River, Suite 103
Novi, MI 48375-2572
(800) 783-3491
(248) 347-3489
Web site: http://www.ameritooldie.com
This magazine serves tool and die makers by presenting articles directly related to the craft. Each issue features news and current information for those wanting to know more about tool and die making.

Tooling and Production
6001 Cochran Road, Suite 104
Solon, OH 44139
(440) 248-1125
e-mail: tooling@aip.com
Web site: http://www.manufacturingcenter.com/tooling
This monthly magazine specializes in the metalworking industry. It provides information on products, industry trends, and techniques.

VIDEOS

Metal Trim Repair & Chrome Preparation

Learn more about working with metal with this informative video. It includes tips on repairing different kinds of metal, as well as techniques to remove scratches and dents in metal.

Patchwork and Metal Finishing

This video will lead you through the basics of how metal is painted, including preparation techniques. It also contains information on working with various types of metals.

SHOE
INDUSTRY
WORKER

Before factories and machines made shoes, people would go to cobblers to have shoes made for them. Handmade shoes were commonplace. It wasn't until 1874, when Charles Goodyear Jr. invented the welt stitcher, that shoes began to be mass-produced. The welt stitcher made possible the production of shoes by a machine. Although there are still people who make shoes by hand, it is much more common to purchase shoes that were made in a factory.

Even though mass production of shoes has lessened the need for cobblers, people are still needed to help construct shoes. The job of a shoe industry worker is to make footwear out of leather and other materials with the help of modern machinery. If you have an interest in working with leather or a fascination with current footwear styles and trends, becoming a shoe industry worker would allow you to combine your interests with your job.

Job Duties

A single pair of shoes may have up to 280 different parts. The job of a shoe industry worker is to put these pieces together to make a functional pair of shoes. Many different machines are used to help. In fact, there can be as many as 150 different machine steps. This means that shoe industry workers must know how to use the many different machines.

The term "shoe industry worker" refers to the many positions available in the industry. Each pair of shoes made in a factory is handled by many different people. An upper-leather sorter goes through pieces of leather and chooses the ones that will be made into shoes. A cut-out-and-marking machine operator cuts the leather into properly sized

A shoe industry worker cleans molds used for creating shoe soles.

pieces. He or she also prepares the leather for sewing by punching holes and marking where the stitching needs to be. Then the materials are given to the standard machine stitchers to assemble. Sometimes they stitch the parts of the shoe together. Other times glue, staples, or another adhesive is used. Then, the shoes are laced, made into different sizes, given insoles, and worked on by many other people before they're ready to be sold. Each person in a shoe factory has a very specific task.

Even in factories in which nonleather shoes are made, there are many different workers whose functions vary. It is still very similar to leather-shoe production, except that the machines need to accommodate materials other than leather. The manufacturing process for nonleather shoes is a bit simpler, though, because the fabric does not need to be inspected, and it can be cut in layers, which is not a possibility when working with leather.

If you're more interested in working with a product from start to finish, you should consider becoming a custom shoemaker. Custom shoemakers assemble shoes by hand or with machines, but they are involved in the whole process. Custom shoemakers usually have a knowledge of shoe repair, too. Considering the ease with which people can buy manufactured shoes, having more skills can only be good for a custom shoemaker.

Education and Training

Even if a person has no knowledge of shoemaking, he or she could start in the shoe-production industry easily. Beginners are trained by employers to work with the different machines. A typical procedure may require a trainee to work with another employee until he or she has mastered a task. Before one can become a custom shoemaker, however, he or she has to be skilled in making shoes.

A good skill to have before getting into this profession is the ability to sew and work a sewing machine. Even if this skill is not required, it can be helpful. Experience working with machines is also a plus. Employers will be looking for some skills that are related to shoe manufacturing.

There are some vocational schools that offer shoe-making and repair classes. In these classes, students learn the basic skills needed to make shoes, such as cutting, dyeing, and stitching leather. Some programs also teach the basics of running a small business.

Salary

Salaries in this industry vary slightly depending on which aspect of shoe production you get into. The median annual salary for both shoe repairers and shoemakers who use machines is $19,000.

Pros and Cons

Learning to manage the machines that are used in a shoe factory will give you the skills needed to cross over into other industries, such as clothing manufacturing and rubber goods

Shoe factory workers are responsible for operating complicated machinery. Having a knowledge of these machines makes it easier to cross over into other industries.

manufacturing. These skills are valued and used in many industries, so finding a different job would be considerably easier than if you did not have experience working with machines.

If you decide to become a custom shoemaker, you may have the opportunity to start your own business or work for a small business. Either option will give you the freedom to oversee production from start to finish, which is important if you're the kind of person who enjoys seeing the fruits of your labor.

Did You Know?

Orthopedic and therapeutic shoemakers are people who make or modify shoes according to a doctor's recommendation. This profession requires more training than is needed for other shoe industry jobs, and the demand for orthopedic and therapeutic shoemakers is greater, especially in areas where there are many elderly people. Plus, the satisfaction of knowing that you can help someone walk more easily may be all you need to consider this career.

Considering the advancement of technology, jobs in shoe factories are expected to decline in the coming years. Many of the tasks that are required of people will be done by machines that are capable of doing some tasks more quickly. Not everyone is well suited to factory work. Machines can be dangerous, so concentration is a key quality in a factory worker. Since the skills you'll obtain on the job are transferable to other industries, finding a job should never be too difficult.

FOR MORE INFORMATION

ASSOCIATIONS

Fashion Footwear Association of New York
1414 Avenue of the Americas, Suite 203
New York, NY 10019
(212) 751-6422
e-mail: info@ffany.org
Web site: http://www.ffany.org
This nonprofit organization serves the footwear industry by organizing footwear trade shows, which bring together people and companies to improve the footwear industry. They also sponsor charitable events and have implemented scholarship programs.

Footwear Industries of America
1420 K Street NW, Suite 600
Washington, DC 20005
(202) 789-1420
e-mail: info@fia.org
Web site: http://www.fia.org
The Footwear Industries of America exists to help various companies in the footwear industry by promoting better quality shoes, customer service, and safety. They make available statistical, marketing, and fashion publications related to the footwear industry.

Pedorthic Footwear Association
7150 Columbia Gateway Drive, Suite G
Columbia, MD 21046
(410) 381-7278
Web site: http://www.pedorthics.org
The Pedorthic Footwear Association is an organization that represents those involved in the orthopedic footwear industry. It holds

events, conferences, and workshops to teach its members more about pedorthics.

WEB SITES

Shoe Info Net
http://www.shoeinfonet.com
This site houses a wealth of information about upcoming shoe industry events and news. It also includes contact information for many organizations, businesses, and people in the shoe industry.

Shoe Service Industry Network
http://www.shoeservice.net
This site serves as a forum for shoe service workers to interact. The site contains information on manufacturers, shoe repair shops, and links for other related Web sites.

Shoe SMARTS
http://www.shoesmarts.com
This Web site, run by the Shoe Service Institute of America, houses a wealth of information for the consumer to learn more about buying, repairing, and maintaining shoes. It also includes tips on choosing a well-fitting pair of shoes and finding a shoe repairer in your area.

BOOKS

Lawlor, Laurie. *Where Will This Shoe Take You? A Walk Through the History of Footwear*. New York: Walker & Company, 1996.
This book takes the reader on a journey to learn about the different types of, styles of, and uses for footwear through the years.

Rossi, William A., ed. *The Complete Footwear Dictionary*. Melbourne, FL: Krieger Publishing Company, 2000.
This dictionary covers the terms used in the footwear industry. It includes information on materials, fashion, and manufacturing.

Salaman, R.A. *Dictionary of Leatherwork*. New York: Saint Martin's Press, 1999.
This book is a resource to those who work with leather and those who enjoy leatherworking as a hobby. Important terms are explained in this book.

Sterlacci, Francesca. *Leather Apparel Design*. Albany, NY: Delmar Publishers, 1997.
If you are interesting in building clothing from leather, this book will help you learn what you need to know to get started. Basics, such as designing, tanning, and handling leather, are included.

PERIODICALS

American Shoemaking
Shoe Trades Publishing Company
61 Massachusetts Avenue
Arlington, MA 02174
(617) 648-8160
Web site: http://www.shoetrades.com
This bimonthly magazine focuses on educating the reader about current footwear manufacturing news and information. It also contains details about events and conventions for the footwear industry.

Footwear News
7 West 34th Street
New York, NY 10001
(212) 630-4000
Web site: http://www.footwearnews.com
Footwear News is a weekly magazine that focuses on the footwear industry. Information about manufacturers and current trends are included in each issue.

ELECTRICIAN

Try to imagine a day without electricity. How would you wake up in the morning without your trusted alarm clock? How would you get through twenty-four hours without the electricity used to power your microwave, refrigerator, and computer? Without electricity, your life would be drastically different. That is why electricians are an important part of our society. They install and repair all of the electrical devices that you have come to depend on. Heating, air conditioning, lighting, refrigeration, and many other things require the expertise of electricians. Their job is complex and necessary.

Job Duties

When a building is constructed, someone needs to make a plan for the electricity. That means that he or she has to decide where outlets, light fixtures, light switches, circuits, and other electrical devices should be located. The electrician follows blueprints to figure out where to install electrical systems that will be used for lighting, heating, cooling, and even communications.

Electricians work with different kinds of wire to connect these complex electrical systems. This is a difficult task because the wires need to be arranged in a very specific way. The wires must be kept in order so that if a problem occurs, the electrician doing maintenance can come in and easily understand where everything is and fix the problem. Electricians have to be organized individuals in order to do their job properly.

In order for the wires to be installed correctly, electricians have to know what kind of wire to use and the best way to connect the type of wire being used. In office buildings and

A technician uses a oscilloscope to test an electrical system.

other commercial buildings, conduit is used. Conduit is piping or tubing used to protect electrical wires. In homes, plastic-covered wire is used. Wires are then joined by either twisting the ends of the wire together with pliers or soldering the ends together with a soldering gun.

Once the wiring is complete, electricians have to test everything to ensure that it was installed correctly and that the electricity is working as it should. They use machines called ohmmeters, voltmeters, and oscilloscopes.

Maintenance electricians must have the same skills as regular electricians, but their duties are a little different. They perform maintenance work on electrical systems in office buildings, residential communities, factories, and other places that need a person on staff to make sure that the electricity is always working correctly. Maintenance electricians fix things when needed, but they are also responsible for making sure that electrical systems get replaced before they break. Depending on where the maintenance electrician works, he or she may be asked to update the wire in a home or repair electrical equipment in a factory. Generally, though, maintenance electricians spend their time checking equipment and practicing preventative measures to keep the electrical systems from breaking unexpectedly.

Education and Training

To become an electrician, you can learn the trade informally by helping an experienced electrician, or you can enroll in an apprenticeship program. As an electrician's assistant, you'll learn safety practices, which are very important. You'll also learn to install and connect wires. As you learn more, you'll be given more responsibility.

Apprenticeship programs work much differently. This training is very comprehensive and will teach you all you need to know to practice the trade in four to five years. Participating in one of these programs will also increase your chances of finding a job because employers know that the trainees will be knowledgeable.

An electrician checks the wiring in a fuse box.

You can start obtaining the skills you'll need to become an electrician right now. Science classes are helpful, as are shop classes. You have to have an understanding of the way electricity works to be able to safely perform your job. You'll also need to read blueprints, so those math classes will definitely come in handy.

Most states require a person to get a license before he or she can officially become an electrician. A test is usually given, with questions ranging from safety precautions to electrical theory.

Salary

An electrician with minimal experience could expect to make $31,000 per year. That is the national average for electricians who have up to two years of experience. A more experienced electrician, with four years in the profession, would make an average base salary of $44,000 per year.

Pros and Cons

No matter where you live, you'll be able to find work as an electrician or a maintenance electrician. Also, there will always be a demand for skilled electricians. As long as there is electricity, there will be a need for people to install electrical systems, test them, and repair them.

Electricians often have to work in uncomfortable or cramped surroundings. They also must stand for long periods of time, and the potential for injury is high. Electricians must be extra careful because electricity can be dangerous, even fatal. There are strict safety guidelines that electricians have to adhere to, or they risk serious injury.

Maintenance electricians sometimes work unusual hours. They generally have on-call hours, which means they have to have a clear schedule during certain hours, in case something needs to be fixed. Electricity is very important to most people, so if something isn't working, they probably want to have it fixed right away.

Did You Know?

Electrocution is a major cause of construction-related deaths. Many workers have been seriously injured, or even died, from not taking the proper precautions. The results of an electric shock can range from a slight tingle to cardiac arrest or a heart attack. What steps can you take to avoid injury? Always keep in mind how close you are working to a powerline. Powerlines are chock-full of electricity, and if you touch one, or even if something that you're touching touches it, you can be seriously injured.

FOR MORE INFORMATION

ASSOCIATIONS

National Electrical Contractors Association
3 Bethesda Metro Center, Suite 1100
Bethesda, MD 20814
(301) 657-3110
Web site: http://www.necanet.org

The National Electrical Contractors Association is an organization that helps those in the industry and those who want to learn more about electrical construction. It publishes informative publications, such as *Electrical Contractor* magazine and has chapters around the world.

North American Electric Reliability Council (NERC)
Princeton Forrestal Village
116-390 Village Boulevard
Princeton, NJ 08540-5731
(609) 452-8060
e-mail: info@nerc.com
Web site: http://www.nerc.com
NERC is a nonprofit organization that was founded in 1968. It works to ensure reliable electricity in North America.

The United States Department of Energy
1000 Independence Avenue SW
Washington, DC 20585
(800) dial-DOE (342-5363)
Web site: http://www.energy.gov
The United States Department of Energy is a governmental organization that strives to provide and maintain a reliable energy system. It is concerned with environmental issues and minimizing environmental waste.

WEB SITES

electrician.com
http://www.electrician.com
This Web site caters to electricians and those who want to learn more about what it's like to be one. It includes articles, a bulletin board, and links to learn more.

Electricity.com
http://www.electricity.com
Check this site for all current electricity-related news.

Electricity Forum
http://www.electricityforum.com
This site caters to the electrical industry by providing up-to-date news and information about publications that are related to this field of work. Check out the industry links to learn more about the electrical industry.

BOOKS

Donnelly, Karen J. *Electrician*. Mankato, MN: Capstone Press, 2001.
This book helps the reader explore a career as an electrician. Topics include job responsibilities, qualifications, and helpful interests.

Gibilisco, Stan. *Teach Yourself Electricity and Electronics*. New York: McGraw-Hill Professional Book Group, 1997.
This guide for beginners teaches the basics of electricity and electronics. It provides information on the science of electricity, as well as wireless communication and the Internet.

Lytle, Elizabeth Stewart. *Careers as an Electrician*. New York: The Rosen Publishing Group, Inc., 1999.
This book explores the careers available for electricians. It describes the steps that must be taken in order to become an electrician.

Matt, Stephen R. *Electricity and Basic Electronics*. Tinley Park, IL: Goodgeart-Wilcox Publisher, 1998.
This book is easy to understand and provides informative text and illustrations to learn more about electricity and electronics. Those interested in a career as an electrician will benefit from the theories and fundamentals that are covered in this book.

PERIODICALS

Electrical Contractor
3 Bethesda Metro Center, Suite 1100
Bethesda, MD 20814-5372
(301) 657-3110
Web site: http://www.ecmag.com

This magazine is distributed for free to all known electrical contractors. It includes statistics and research, as well as guides to products.

Electrical Line
Subscription Department
3105 Benbow Road
West Vancouver, BC V7V 3E1
(604) 922-5516
e-mail: sales@electricalline.com
Web site: http://www.electricalline.com
Electrical Line magazine is a bimonthly publication for electricians operating in Canada. It includes industry news, product information, and articles about the industry.

VIDEOS

Made Easy: Electrical **(1985)**
Warner Home Video
This video will provide you with the basics so that you can learn about being an electrician and making repairs on your home electrical systems.

JEWELER AND JEWELRY REPAIRER

Jewelers and jewelry repairers are responsible for crafting and mending beautiful pieces of jewelry out of gold, silver, gemstones, and other precious materials. The idea of wearing jewelry as an accessory dates back very far. You've surely seen illustrations of cave dwellers wearing accessories fashioned from bones and shells. You've also probably seen the beautiful, intricate gold jewelry of the ancient Egyptians. Jewelry has been around for many years, and its popularity shows no sign of letting up; neither do the job opportunities for jewelers and jewelry repairers.

Job Duties

Jewelers come up with ideas for pieces or create jewelry from someone else's design. An interest in jewelry design is helpful for this part of the job. An ability to draw well also helps. This job takes a lot of creativity and is best suited for someone with a background in art.

Whether or not the jeweler has designed his or her own piece, the steps taken to create jewelry are the same. He or she begins by making a mold. The mold is made from a carving in metal or wax. Plaster is poured inside to make the mold that will be used to make the piece of jewelry. Precious metals, such as silver, gold, and platinum, are then melted and poured into the mold. This is what will become the metal model. When the metal is cooled, special touches may be added. For example, the piece may need to be filed or polished before it is complete.

Jewelry repairers have a much different job. They work with pieces that have been damaged in some way. Sometimes they will replace a lost stone or resize a ring. Other days they may be replacing clasps or restringing beads.

Jewelers may own their retail stores where they make and sell their creations. It has become less popular, however, to do this. It is more common for jewelers to work in a jewelry store owned by another person. In such retail stores, it is common for the owner to purchase the jewelry from a wholesaler instead of relying on an in-house jeweler. In a retail store, the jeweler is usually responsible for working with customers, helping them find the kind of jewelry they are looking for. It is also not unusual to be expected to complete cash and credit transactions.

If your main interest is in the design aspect of jewelry, you might want to consider working as a jewelry designer. Jewelry design has become more recognized as an art form, and many artists have turned to jewelry making to express their creativity. In 1990, the American Jewelry Design Council was founded because people wanted jewelry to be considered more of an art form than it had been previously.

Education and Training

It is possible to enroll in classes in community colleges and trade schools to learn jewelry making and repair. These classes are good places to learn about different precious metals and gemstones and the different techniques that are used to create jewelry.

A jeweler cuts diamond facets at a finishing shop.

Apprenticeships and on-the-job training are also useful if you want to pursue a career in this field. These options would give you hands-on training. After two years as an apprentice, you would be required to take a test before you can become a jeweler. Questions on the test cover subjects like gemstone identification, casting a mold, and engraving.

While you are considering this career, you might want to consider taking an art or industrial arts class. Art classes will help you decide if jewelry design is something that

you're interested in. Industrial arts classes will give you experience working with machines. Jewelers work with many different machines, most of them requiring a lot of hand-eye coordination and good eyesight.

You might even want to consider getting a part-time job in a jewelry store to see how you like it. Even though you wouldn't be crafting pieces of jewelry, you'll still get a feel for the atmosphere of a jewelry store and be able to decide if this is a career you want to begin.

Salary

Depending on what kind of work you do, salaries vary greatly. Some jewelers who design and create their own jewelry attract famous clients and can do very well for themselves. But for most, jewelry design is a fine art and is a difficult field to earn a living in. According to the *Occupational Outlook Handbook*, the 1998 median annual salary for jewelers was $24,000. The job of jewelry repairer starts at minimum wage.

A jewelry maker solders metal. Goggles must be worn for safety.

Did You Know?

The House of Winston is a jewelry store with branches in a few cities, including New York and Paris. They are known for lending very expensive pieces of jewelry to stars to wear to events, such as the Oscars. The most expensive loan ever made to a performer for the Oscars was to Whoopi Goldberg. She borrowed $41 million worth of jewels for the 1999 Academy Awards, including a ring worth $15 million.

Pros and Cons

The perks and drawbacks of this profession depend on the field that you're interested in. If you decide to design jewelry, you'll surely get extreme satisfaction from seeing your designs made into beautiful pieces of jewelry, whether or not you actually made them.

If you decide to be self-employed, which is very common—about 50 percent of jewelers are self-employed—you'll be able to choose your work environment. You may choose to work from your home, or you may decide to own a small shop and work from there.

No matter what you decide to pursue, jewelers and jewelry repairers often have to sit for a long time while working on their pieces. They also must have the ability to concentrate for long periods of time on the task at hand. If one is not paying close attention, injury can occur. Some of the machines can get very hot, and others are sharp. Safety is very important in this field.

FOR MORE INFORMATION

ASSOCIATIONS

Jewelers of America
52 Vanderbilt Avenue, 19th Floor
New York, NY 10017
(646) 658-0256
Web site: http://www.jewelers.org
Jewelers of America is the largest trade organization for retail jewelers. Its goal is to educate the consumer about fine jewelry and serve jewelry professionals. The organization makes available information about jewelry, such as care and cleaning, selecting jewelry, and choosing a jeweler.

Jewelry Information Center
19 West 44th Street
New York, NY 10036
(212) 398-2319
Web site: http://jic.polygon.net
The Jewelry Information Center can provide you with more information about the careers available in the jewelry industry.

Manufacturing Jewelers and Suppliers of America
45 Royal Little Drive
Providence, RI 02904
(800) 444-MJSA
e-mail: mjsa@mjsainc.com
Web site: http://www.mjsainc.org
The MJSA is an organization that holds educational trade shows, provides information, and publishes *AJM* (Authority on Jewelry Manufacturing) magazine. Check its Web site to learn about its work and get its newsletter.

WEB SITES

Ganoskin.com
http://www.ganoksin.com
Browse this site to find articles that pertain to jewelry. You may also use the site explorer to read tips from jewelers about jewelry making and look at the artist galleries the site has.

Jewelry Central
http://www.jewelrycentral.com
This site has much to offer about jewelry, including how to choose a gem, where to go to find what you're looking for, and how to care for your jewelry. This site also has an extensive Frequently Asked Questions section to help answer your jewelry-related questions.

BOOKS

Dubbs-Ball, Joanne. *Costume Jewelers: The Golden Age of Design*. Atglen, PA: Schiffer Publishing, Limited, 1997.
Jewelry collectors and enthusiasts will find this book to be of interest. In it, you will find information on the design and manufacture of costume jewelry.

Hardy, R. Allen. *The Jewelry Repair Manual*. Mineloa, NY: Dover Publications, Incorporated, 1996.
This manual teaches the basics of jewelry repair and also appeals to the skilled jewelry repairperson by including some of the more advanced techniques.

Jarvis, Charles. *Jewelry Manufacture and Repair*. Wappingers Falls, NY: N. A. G. Press, 1990.
This book explains the techniques used by skilled jewelry makers.

Revere, Alan. *Art of Jewelry Making: Classic and Original Designs*. New York: Sterling Publishing Company, Incorporated, 1999.
Instructions for jewelry-making projects are explained in this book. It also includes biographical information on well-known artists.

Spears, Therese. *Flash Jewelry Making and Repair Techniques*. Boulder, CO: Promenade Publishing, 1990.
This book provides tips and information on making and repairing your own jewelry. Check it out to learn more.

Wallace, Mary. *I Can Make Jewelry*. Toronto, ON: Owl Books, 1997.
Clear photographs and easy instructions help to teach the beginner about jewelry making. This book also includes tips to make simple pieces of jewelry.

PERIODICALS

Jewelry Crafts
58 South Piney Plains Circle
The Woodlands, TX 77382
e-mail: jwlrymag@flex.net
Web site: http://www.jewelrycrafts.com
If you're interested in learning to make your own jewelry, check out *Jewelry Crafts*. Each issue of this magazine contains how-to information for different projects, such as beading, silversmithing, and clay projects.

Modern Jeweler
445 Broad Hollow Road
Melville, NY 11747
(631) 845-2700
Web site: http://www.modernjeweler.com
Modern Jeweler is a style magazine that focuses on jewelry. Those in the industry look to this magazine to find out the current trends.

Professional Jeweler
1500 Walnut Street, Suite 1200
Philadelphia, PA 19102
e-mail: askus@professionaljeweler.com
Web site: http://www.professionaljeweler.com
This magazine, published monthly, brings you information about jewelry. Each issue contains articles featuring news pertaining to the jewelry industry. Go to the Web site to sign up for a free newsletter and check statistics about jewelry.

VIDEOS

Jewelry from Recyclables
This crafts video will teach you to make your own jewelry from recyclables. You'll learn tips and tricks to make your own jewelry.

Master Artisans: Jewelry Making Techniques
Polymer Video
Check out this video to learn the different techniques for making jewelry.

[12]

TAILOR AND DRESSMAKER

Clothing is an important part of our society. People practice self-expression by the clothes they wear. People make careers out of studying clothing and fashion. And tailors and dressmakers are the people who make these articles of clothing for others to wear.

The practice of wearing clothing began as a way to keep warm and survive extreme weather. Through the years the practice has changed drastically. People now choose their clothing depending on their taste and style. It is no longer just about survival anymore. The fashion industry is big business, and tailors and dressmakers are an important part of the industry.

Job Duties

Typically, tailors construct clothing for men, and dressmakers make clothing for women. It is possible for a tailor or dressmaker to start and finish the same article of clothing, but that is typically reserved for people who work in smaller shops. If seeing something through to completion is what you're interested in, you might want to obtain a job in a small shop, rather than a large factory, or construct your own clothes as a hobby during your free time.

In a larger facility, such as a factory or large store, different tasks are handled by different people. For example, you may be given the responsibility of sewing sleeves onto a garment or putting in shoulder pads. Other work, such as patternmaking and measuring fabric, would be handled by other workers.

If you worked as a tailor or dressmaker in a bridal shop or large department store, you would be required to make alterations. It is very common for upscale stores to employ

This bridal shop dressmaker is ready to handle the many requests for alterations she receives on an average day.

a tailor or dressmaker, in case a customer needs something altered to fit better.

The first step in creating an article of clothing is the choice of fabric. There are many fabrics as well as colors to choose from. The customer then needs to be measured accurately for size. A pattern is chosen, and the fabric is cut to match it. Then, all the pieces are sewn together. The customer then tries the piece of clothing. Any ill-fitting areas are corrected and the garment is finished.

Education and Training

If you've already begun your own sewing projects, you're on the right track. The ability to sew is a necessary skill for a tailor or dressmaker, so if you're considering this profession, you will have to learn to sew. Your school may offer art classes that incorporate sewing, or you can take a sewing class at a local recreation center.

It is best to have a love of fashion to enter this field. You'll be required to help customers pick out styles that best suit them and that are current. A knowledge of different kinds of fabric is also helpful because they are the backbone of your creations.

If you're interested in starting your own business, you can begin by sewing clothing and selling to local shops or to your friends. If you can build a base of people who want to purchase things from you, you may be able to open a store and sell your clothing from there.

If you're already skilled in sewing, you can obtain a job as an alterer in a factory or large store. A job like this will give you more experience working in the field and will possibly open up more career opportunities.

A dressmaker sews a costume for the Shakespeare Festival in Stratford, Ontario.

Salary

These days, tailors and dressmakers make an average of approximately $19,500 per year. If, however, you decide that you're more interested in sewing your own designs, your profit would be based on how much you charge for your creations. It is not unusual for a tailor or dressmaker to pick up additional freelance projects to make extra money.

Pros and Cons

If you already enjoy sewing and creating your own articles of clothing, becoming a tailor or dressmaker could be the ideal job because you would be able to practice your hobby and get paid for it. You will also be surrounded by like-minded people who share your interest.

If you decide to get a job in a large factory, you may find the noise from the machines disturbing. However, most factories abide by building codes to ensure that the workplace is clean and safe.

You must be very skilled to obtain a job in this field, but if sewing is your passion, getting a job should be easy. If you're interested in utilizing your creative side, this may be the career for you!

Did You Know?

Elias Howe is often credited with inventing the sewing machine because he held patents for it in 1844. But models had been built long before that—the earliest functional model in France, in 1830.

Bathelemy Thimonnier created the first working sewing machine. People were afraid that the sewing machine would eliminate the need for hand stitchers, causing people to lose their jobs, and Thimonnier's factory was burned down and his machines destroyed. He fled to England to escape any further persecution, but he is truly the inventor of the first working sewing machine.

Fun Fact

Television shows, movies, and theater productions all rely on a wardrobe person to supply the outfits for the production. Sometimes this person is called a wardrobe coordinator, wardrobe assistant, or costume designer. Some productions are easier than others to find wardrobe for, especially if they're set in current times. But many productions take place in another era,

(continued on next page)

and that's when the skills of a wardrobe person are really tested. He or she must find costumes that fit the period in which the production takes place. Then he or she must alter them to fit the actors and actresses. If costumes are not easily obtainable, the wardrobe coordinator must create the costumes from scratch. This is the ideal job for a skilled tailor or dressmaker with an interest in television, movies, and theater.

FOR MORE INFORMATION

ASSOCIATIONS

American Apparel and Footwear Association
1601 N. Kent Street, Suite 1200
Arlington, VA 22209
(800) 520-2262
Web site: http://www.americanapparel.org
This organization was founded in 2000 by the merger of the American Apparel Manufacturers Association, the Fashion Association, and the Footwear Industries of America. It represents the apparel industry by promoting education, providing news and information, and making resources about the apparel industry available.

British Columbia Apparel Industry Association
110-355 Burrard Street
Vancouver, BC V6C 2G8
(604) 689-2775
Web site: http://www.apparel-bc.org
This Canadian organization serves as a liaison between government, media, and apparel industry workers in matters concerning the apparel industry. Its meetings allow members to share ideas and discuss issues, such as wages, trends, and labor.

WEB SITES

101 Sewing Links
http://www.sharewareplace.com/101/101sew.shtml
This site is a directory of sewing-related information.

Sewing World
http://www.sewingworld.com
Sewing World brings you a wealth of information about sewing, such as up-to-date sewing news, discussion boards, and downloadable embroidery files.

BOOKS

Betzina, Sandra. *Fabric Savvy: The Essential Advice for Every Sewer*. Newtown, CT: Taunton Press, Incorporated, 1998.
This handy reference book will teach all you need to know about choosing fabrics for your creations.

Carr, Harold. *Technology in Clothing Manufacture*. London: Blackwell Scientific Publications, Limited, 1994.
Check out this book to learn about clothing manufacturing, including information on the machines used, methods for cutting and sewing, and the use of computers.

Rudman, Jack. *Dressmaking*. Syosset, NY: National Learning Corporation, 1994.
If you're interested in becoming a dressmaker, this book will help you prepare for the tests that may be required of you. Sample exams give you a taste of what to expect.

Rudman, Jack. *Tailor*. Syosset, NY: National Learning Corporation, 1994. This guide will get you ready for your exam if you're going to be taking a competency test to prove your tailoring knowledge.

Saunders, Jan. *Sewing for Dummies.* Indianapolis, IN: I D G Books Worldwide, 1999.
Step-by-step instructions are paired with informative pictures to help you get started in sewing. This book ranges from the most simple aspects of sewing to the more complex, to give you a wide range of sewing instructions.

Sykes, Barbara W. *The Business of Sewing: How to Start, Maintain and Achieve Success*. Chino Hills, CA: Collins Publications, 1992.
This is a guide to starting your own sewing business. Topics such as developing a business plan and choosing employees are covered.

PERIODICALS

Sewing Savvy
23 Old Pecan Road
Big Sandy, TX 75755
e-mail: editor@sewingsavvy.com
Web site: http://www.sewingsavvy.com
Sewing enthusiasts look to this magazine to get tips on sewing, as well as informative articles, free patterns, and regular features. This magazine will surely be of help if you love to sew!

Threads
The Taunton Press, Inc.
63 South Main Street
P.O. Box 5506
Newtown, CT 06470
(202) 426-8171
Web site: http://www.taunton.com/th/th/index.htm
Threads is a magazine for those in the garment industry. Each issue includes articles to help tailors and dressmakers learn more about their craft. Topics covered range from fabric to helpful sewing and designing tips.

VIDEOS

Sewing Seams Simple for Teens (1995)
If you're a beginner, look no further for a video to help you learn to sew. It's perfect for those just starting out.

Speed Sewing: Ten Super Tips
This video will be most helpful if you already know how to sew. It provides tips on improving the speed of your sewing.

GLOSSARY

apprenticeship The process by which a person receives instruction on how to perform a job.

commercial building A structure that is used for business purposes.

commission Getting paid a percentage of a sale as salary.

commodity Something that has a benefit, usually financial.

conduit Material that is used to protect wires or cable.

freelancer A person who is paid for performing a task but is not bound to a long-term agreement.

garnish A decorative touch sometimes used in food preparation.

hydroponic gardening A way of growing flora using nutrient solutions instead of soil.

illustration A drawing used to clarify something.

install The process by which something is adjusted or put into place for use.

intricacies Things that are complex or complicated.

journeyman An experienced worker who takes on and trains an apprentice.

livelihood The occupation by which a person is financially supported.

machinist A person skilled in operating machines or machine tools.

maintenance Upkeep to ensure that something is kept in proper condition.

multisensory Using many bodily senses.

musket A type of shoulder gun that was used in the late sixteenth century up until the eighteenth century.

niche A position for which one is well suited.

patent A governmental grant that is given to an inventor, granting him or her the sole right to use the product for profit.

pesticide A chemical that is used to kill insects and other pests.

photosynthesis The process by which plants use carbon dioxide, water, and sunlight to produce carbohydrates and oxygen.

residential building A structure used for living purposes.

stamina Ability to withstand long periods of mental or physical fatigue; endurance.

technology The application of science to industry or commerce.

trade An occupation that requires skilled labor.

variation The extent toward which something can be different; change.

INDEX

A

apprenticeships, 12, 22, 23, 24, 45, 89, 109, 119

art, 31, 32, 33, 35, 37, 66, 76, 80, 118, 119–121, 131

auto mechanic, 53-63
  education/training needed, 56–58
  job duties, 54–56
  pros and cons, 58–59
  salary, 58
  similar professions, 60

B

blueprints, 21, 23, 86, 89, 107, 110

COOL CAREERS WITHOUT COLLEGE

C

carpenter, 8, 20–30, 43
 education/training needed, 22–24
 job duties, 21–22
 pros and cons, 25–27
 salary, 24–25
cobbler, 96, 97
construction worker, 42–52
 education/training needed, 45
 job duties, 43–45
 pros and cons, 46–49
 salary, 45
 women as, 48
contractor, 43–44, 45
Crapper, Thomas, 15

D

doll collecting, 75–76, 80
doll maker, 75–84
 education/training needed, 78–79
 job duties, 76–78
 pros and cons, 80
 salary, 79

E

electrician, 43, 106–115
 education/training needed, 109
 job duties, 107–109
 pros and cons, 111
 salary, 111
Empire State Building, 48

G

gardener, 8, 64–74
 aquatic, 69
 education/training needed, 66–68
 job duties, 65–66
 pros and cons, 68–69
 salary, 68
Goodyear, Charles, Jr., 96
greenhouse workers, 65

H

Howe, Elias, 133
hydroponic gardening, 70

J

jeweler/jewelry repairer, 116–126
 education/training needed, 118–121
 job duties, 117–118
 pros and cons, 122–123
 salary, 121
jewelry designer, 118, 119–121, 122
journeyman, 12

L

landscape laborers, 65
lawn service workers, 65–66
Lyon, Norma "Duffy," 36

P

pesticides, 67

plumber, 9–19, 22, 43
  education/training needed,
    11–12
  job duties, 10–11
  pros and cons, 14–15
  salary, 12–14

R
Raggedy Ann and Andy, 81

S
safety, 10, 23, 24, 27, 49, 59, 67,
    90, 110, 111, 112, 123
sculptor, 31–41
  education/training needed,
    34–35
  job duties, 32–34
  pros and cons, 37
  salary, 35–37
self-employment, 15, 26, 33, 46,
    122, 131
shoe industry worker, 96–105
  education/training needed,
    99–100
  job duties, 97–99
  for orthopedic/therapeutic
    shoes, 102
  pros and cons, 100–102
  salary, 100

T
tailor/dressmaker, 127–137
  education/training needed, 131

job duties, 128–129
  pros and cons, 132
  salary, 132
Thimonnier, Bathelemy, 133
tool and die maker, 85–95
  education/training needed, 89
  job duties, 86–89
  pros and cons, 90
  salary, 90
  similar professions, 91

U
U.S. Department of Labor, 27, 42,
    54, 90

W
Whitney, Eli, 87
woodworking, 8, 20, 21, 24

About the Author

Joy Paige works and resides in New York. She enjoys many hobbies, including woodworking, painting, and swing dancing. She spends most of her free time with her parrot, aptly named Bird.

Photo Credits

Cover © SuperStock; pp. 9, 13 © Dave Thompson/Life File/PhotoDisc; p. 10 © Tony Savino/The Image Works; pp. 20, 25 © The Image Works; p. 22 © Jon Riley/Index Stock Imagery, Inc.; p. 23 © Mark Gibson/Index Stock Imagery, Inc.; pp. 31, 32 courtesy of Liz Lomax; p. 34 © E.B. McGovern/*East Valley Tribune*/AP Wide World; p. 36 © Timothy O'Keefe/Index Stock Imagery, Inc.; pp. 42, 44 © Dick Blume/Syracuse Newspapers/The Image Works; p. 47 © SuperStock; pp. 53, 59 © Robert Brimson/FPG International; p. 55 © Francisco Cruz/Superstock; p. 57 © Wayne H. Chasan/Image Bank; p. 60 © Phillip Spears/PhotoDisc; pp. 64, 66 © Pictor; p. 70 © EyeWire; pp. 75, 77 © David J. Phillip/AP Wide World; p. 78 © Richard T. Nowitz/Corbis; p. 81 © The Purcell Team/Corbis; pp. 85, 88 © Macduff Everton/Corbis; p. 91 © Bret McCown/*The Havre Daily News*/AP Wide World; pp. 96, 98 © Danny Lehman/Corbis; p. 101 © Robin Moyer/Timepix; pp. 106, 110 © Arthur S. Aubry/PhotoDisc; p.108 © Eye Uhiquitous/Kevin Wilton/Corbis; pp. 116, 119 © Charles O'Rear/Corbis; p. 120 © Leslie Harris/Index Stock Imagery, Inc.; pp. 127, 129 © Miles Schuster/SuperStock; p. 130 © Kelly-Mooney Photography/Corbis.

Design and Layout

Evelyn Horovicz